THE
Data Wrangler's
HANDBOOK

THE
Data Wrangler's
HANDBOOK

SIMPLE TOOLS FOR POWERFUL RESULTS

KYLE BANERJEE

ALA
Neal-Schuman
Chicago 2019

Kyle Banerjee has wrangled data for diverse purposes in academic, government, and nonprofit environments since 1996. A firm believer that understanding people is the key to building services of the future from the systems and data of the past, his professional interests revolve around understanding workflows and identifying opportunities in data previously thought inconsistent or incomplete. Kyle has published four other books and numerous articles on a variety of topics related to applying technology in library settings.

Extensive effort has gone into ensuring the reliability of the information in this book; however, the publisher makes no warranty, express or implied, with respect to the material contained herein.

ISBNs
978-0-8389-1909-5 (paper)
978-0-8389-1913-2 (PDF)
978-0-8389-1910-1 (ePub)
978-0-8389-1911-8 (Kindle)

Library of Congress Control Number: 2019024258

Book design by Kimberly Thornton in the Skolar Altin, Vista, and Archer typefaces. Cover image © zaie/Adobe Stock, icons © vasabii/Adobe Stock.

⊗ This paper meets the requirements of ANSI/NISO Z39.48–1992 (Permanence of Paper).

Printed in the United States of America

23 22 21 20 19   5 4 3 2 1

CONTENTS

FIGURES

TABLES

ACKNOWLEDGMENTS

The subject of making technology more accessible is one that's been near and dear to me for many years, but this book never would have been written had it not been for a number of individuals. Bonnie Parks has been willing to share experiences that remind me why most people—especially women—still get left behind when it comes to technology despite initiatives to help people become more proficient. As I began work on this book, Julie Swierczek, Erica Findley, and Rosie Le Faive also made suggestions about what sort of topics should be covered. I hope they and others will continue to raise their voices to draw attention to what areas we need to work on.

Making technology accessible is all about identifying the simple and powerful ideas and tools from an overwhelming sea of choices. David Forero is one of the technologists who's especially good at doing that. He excels at describing complex ideas in plain English, which you'll benefit from directly when you learn about formats in chapter 3, but his influence can also be seen throughout the book.

I also would like to thank ALA Neal-Schuman for their support over the years. Many people have asked why I don't simply post what I write on the web. The reason is simple—the result you see wouldn't be nearly as good without their hard work.

Finally, I would like to thank Mark Dahl. He convinced me that things are much easier than they look and that obstacles people find blocking their paths exist more in their minds than in reality. It never would have occurred to me that writing a book or hiking miles through wilderness to climb a mountain and ski off the top were reasonable things for mere mortals to do had he not approached me years ago to do both with him.

My hope is that this book will help others realize how achievable many intimidating-sounding data wrangling tasks are, and that people will help others know these things are much easier than they appear.

Virtually everyone needs to wrangle data. Your spreadsheet

software might not offer a way to select the rows you want. If you can get the rows you want, you might not be able to sort them the way you need because the names or other fields you wanted to sort on weren't entered in a consistent format. When you export your spreadsheet in delimited format so you can load it into other programs, you might experience difficulties if fields contain line breaks, HTML (HyperText Markup Language), or other data that won't load properly. You might have to restructure and remap data so a new system can understand it. In addition to spreadsheets, people often need automated ways to process large numbers of files in a wide variety of formats in complex hierarchies or interact with online systems.

If these tasks sound intimidating, this book is for you. You will understand everything in this book even if you have no special technical knowledge or programming experience. You'll see how easy it is to do things that previously sounded difficult or even impossible using tools that are already on your computer and that a rudimentary knowledge of a few basic but powerful concepts and tools can solve the vast majority of the data challenges you'll ever face.

Data wrangling is relatively easy for two simple reasons. The first is that the vast majority of the information we need to manage and analyze is text. When you hear people talk about manipulating delimited, XML (eXtensible Markup Language), JSON (JavaScript Object Notation), Linked Open Data, RDF (Resource Description Framework) resources, or internal metadata, they are talking about manipulating text. When librarians manipulate MARC (MAchine Readable Cataloging), they convert it to text before making transformations. When you hear people talk about using a REST (Representational State Transfer) API (Application Programming Interface) to interact with a service, they are usually just talking about sending text across a network. When people manipulate internal metadata in binary files, that too is text. When you strip away the confusing jargon, the vast majority of data wrangling librarians do is ultimately about manipulating text you could view in any word processor.

The second reason data wrangling is easy is because the tools you need are already part of modern operating systems. Armed with just rudimentary knowledge of how to use these tools, you can do amazing things with files that are millions of lines long, talk to other systems, and perform tasks in seconds that may have previously seemed impossible. This book will show you how to use simple methods that work on any computer to manage text-based data.

The tools discussed in this book won't solve all your problems, but they will help you solve the vast majority of them fairly easily. To use them, you'll have to access the Command Line Interface (CLI) on your computer. Most people find that little black box intimidating, but here's an analogy that may help. For most people, using a computer is a lot like eating at a restaurant—they use a Graphical User Interface (GUI) to point at what they want, much like you'd select your dinner from a menu. GUIs are great for selecting from limited choices of actions. But sometimes you need something that's not on the menu. You need language to tell the server about food allergies or other special requirements. Or maybe you'd just rather make something at home yourself because it's easier to get what you really wanted. That's what using the CLI is all about.

Every example used in this book will look like something you've seen before or are very likely to see. Think about it like this—to cook for yourself, you need a few basic skills and recipes. Once you understand these fundamental ingredients and methods, you can make simple dishes. Making complicated dishes is mostly a matter of combining these same ingredients and techniques in new ways—a little knowledge goes a long way.

This book is like a basic cookbook for librarians who work with data. To keep things digestible so you can remember what you read and do useful things, the book presents only the most essential information, focusing on what has proven most useful to the author over more than twenty years of wrangling data in a library environment. It will not teach you how to program. Programming is a useful skill, but it requires a lot of extra knowledge and effort that are not necessary for most problems.

This book will help you develop a firm grasp of the fundamentals and enable you to address a wide variety of practical challenges. For example, you will be able to use your regular work or home computer to easily:

- find and fix bad data in a 20 GB file
- repeat a process on all the files in a directory that meet criteria you specify

- extract information from and add information to very large files based on criteria you specify
- retrieve a record over a network, modify, and replace it in three lines
- do many other things you may have thought impossible

If you already have data manipulation skills, you're undoubtedly interested in learning faster and better ways to do things. You've come to the right place. Even if you're already familiar with much of the content in this book, you may find some tools and methods presented here are outside your range of experience. Technology constantly advances, but critical tools and methods developed decades ago when computing power was limited and expensive are enormously useful with large data problems. Likewise, newer tools and methods are indispensable for addressing certain challenges.

As you work your way through the book, the most important thing to do is to understand the core concepts and situations in which they're useful so you'll know which questions to ask when you run into trouble. Don't worry about memorizing syntax—you can always look that up later if you need to.

In all cases, the most important things to understand are introduced at the beginning of each chapter. Subsequent chapters assume you're familiar with this core material, but they will not expect you to understand more sophisticated examples appearing near the ends of the chapters. Rather, those examples are provided for readers interested in extra information about more powerful ways to use things they've just learned.

Chapter 1 helps you take your first steps. You'll learn about your computer environment and about basic concepts that help you navigate any computer environment.

Chapter 2 is the most important chapter in the book. It shows you how you can start applying these concepts right away on the computer you use every day, and how to direct the output of programs to other programs, effectively combining their functionality. It will introduce you to regular expressions— one of the most useful data manipulation concepts. Support for these can be found in a wide variety of software—including word processing and spreadsheet software you already use.

Chapter 3 helps you understand what formats really are so you can use the same simple tools to perform sophisticated operations on delimited text, XML, JSON, and other formats.

Chapter 4 shows you how to simplify problems. In real life, data problems can seem overwhelming. This section provides a few basic techniques for breaking complicated problems into simple steps. It will also show you how to convert formats you're not familiar with into ones you're comfortable with, and how to use simple tools to solve complex problems.

Delimited text is an old but ubiquitous format. Chapter 5 introduces the tools and techniques to address a wide variety of challenges such as line feeds in fields, working with multivalue fields, and what you can do when your data contains delimiter characters.

Chapter 6 helps you learn about XML. Although virtually everyone who works with data has worked with XML, most people find it intimidating because of the sheer number and complexity of technologies required to work with it. This chapter will help you understand how to easily perform powerful tasks with just a bit of knowledge of some simple tools.

Chapter 7 familiarizes you with JSON. Although JSON has historically been only of interest to programmers, this format is frequently used as a simpler alternative to XML, so a little familiarity with it can make your life much easier.

Chapter 8 introduces you to scripting. Scripts are regular text files you can create in any word processor that combine command line instructions, programs, system utilities, and other scripts to create programs customized to meet a very wide variety of needs.

By definition, handbooks are short so that you don't get lost in endless detail. However, some specialized problems are so common for librarians working with data that they're worth discussing specifically. Chapter 9 addresses some of these issues, but also introduces more complexity into examples to help you imagine how you can combine ideas introduced earlier in the book.

After the conclusions (chapter 10), you'll find a section entitled One-Line Wonders that demonstrates how to do what's most important when it comes to viewing, analyzing, and manipulating data. In most cases, the material will seem familiar because it appears in earlier sections. However, there are also instances that use capabilities of commands not discussed elsewhere. Some of the commands listed here are so powerful that entire books have been written on them, and there are many other commands and techniques that can be used to perform tasks shown here. Hopefully, some of the solutions will give you an idea of what power some of these commands have and inspire you to investigate further

All of the chapters have two things in common. The first is that they'll help you tell your computer what you want using words rather than a GUI to extract, analyze, and manipulate data. The second is that they'll help you understand how simple most data problems really are. They'll help you understand that virtually all of the data problems librarians work with ultimately boil down to working with text, and that working with text is easy.

You may wonder what's wrong with using Microsoft Excel or OpenRefine. For many simple tasks, both of these programs are good choices, and Excel is probably the most popular way to work with data. However, neither program is appropriate for non-tabular data or very large files, nor do they lend themselves well towards automation or integration with other processes.

In addition, Excel presents the following challenges:

- It mangles your data. Identifiers, numbers, and dates are particularly at risk because Excel automatically converts data in undesirable ways rendering it corrupted.
- It cannot handle carriage returns within individual fields. Delimited data often contains carriage return or newline characters. Excel treats all data after such characters as the beginning of a new row when it is part of a field.
- It only works with simple tabular data. It does not work with XML, JSON, or delimited data containing multiple levels of delineation. Excel crashes with large files, rendering it useless for a wide variety of projects.
- It has limited analytic and processing tools. Sophisticated operations, especially those involving interaction with other programs, require real programming skills.

OpenRefine is better than Excel because it doesn't mangle data, works with larger files than Excel, has better regular expression support, and has better built-in tools for analyzing and cleaning data. As a GUI program, OpenRefine is one of the better options for working with data, but it still cannot compete with the command line for power, speed, and ease of use.

Don't worry if you're not sure how that intimidating box that people type commands into relates to other files and programs on your computer. Don't even worry if you didn't know how to find the box and feel anxiety just thinking of using it. That's a totally normal reaction to an environment that doesn't give any hints about what you should do next.

People who've never used a command line often ask, "What can you do with it?" This is like asking a handyperson what you can do with tools or a chef what you can do in a kitchen. The answer: it depends on what you plan to do—the whole point of the command line is it allows you to express complex ideas precisely. Everyone's needs are different, so use the examples for ideas about how you might apply tools and concepts to do what's important to you.

As you get started, the main things to keep in mind are:

1. The whole reason computers exist is to wrangle data. Every computer program ever written takes data from somewhere, analyzes or manipulates it, and outputs different data. This means specialized commands that do practically everything you need—normalize dates in one of the columns in a giant file, sophisticated manipulation of structured files, identification of duplicate values—already exist, so you won't have to write programs that perform these tasks. Rather, all you need to do is learn about the programs you'll use the most and how to string them together to do what you need.

2. People find command lines intimidating because they don't give any clues as to what you can do or what you should do next. However, even for beginners, it's often far easier to use commands than a GUI to solve problems. When you're not sure how to perform a task or use a command, typing what you want to do into an internet search engine and adding the word "example" to your search usually brings results that include the commands you need along with examples of how to use them.

3. Working with a command line is a lot like cooking. With very little knowledge, you can do incredible things with a pan, a pot, a knife, and a few utensils. Likewise, you can do amazing things with data if you know a little bit about it and are familiar with a few basic tools. The key is to experiment—failed attempts don't hurt your kitchen or computer in the least, but they do help you figure things out and have more fun.

4. There are usually many ways to accomplish the same task, even when using a single command. In this book, you will normally see only one way to do something. Sometimes, this is in the interest of keeping things simple but sometimes it's just to expose you to another way of thinking. The examples you see may or may not portray the "best" way, so you're encouraged to explore other ways of performing tasks if you feel inclined to look for better methods.

5. To keep the subject matter digestible, only the basic functionality of individual commands is demonstrated in this book. If you find yourself wishing that a particular command could do just a bit more, look online or ask for help because there's a good chance the command already does what you want.

6. It's easier if you just learn what you need as you need it. Learn one command at a time, and don't worry about what you don't know until it prevents you from doing what you want.

So let's get started!

## CHAPTER 1

Getting Started with the Command Line

Modern computer design assumes people use a GUI to interact with them. That's true most of the time, so the command line tends to be hidden and the system doesn't even tell you it exists. But that doesn't mean it's not important. The command line might be your window to the oldest part of the system, but it's also your ticket to a better and easier way to do all kinds of work. Later in this book, you'll learn to do amazing things with a single line of code and make short work of enormous projects with just a few lines. In fact, you'll find a section towards the end called One-Line Wonders that shows you how to do dozens of common tasks in just one line.

All examples in this book will focus on command prompts that you can use on any Windows, Mac, or Linux computer. Every now and then, there will be an example where you might need to do something a little different on a Mac—this will be pointed out when it's the case.

Preparing your system so you can use the command prompt can be one of the most intimidating parts of the entire process, but don't be discouraged. The instructions are strange and archaic, but you only have to complete them once. It is not necessary to memorize the process or try to learn anything from it. There will be plenty of opportunity to learn much more interesting things soon!

Finding the Command Line

Mac

If you have a Mac, you'll use a program called Terminal. It's located within the Utilities folder that is found in the Applications folder, which can be accessed directly by typing COMMAND-SHIFT-U. Alternatively, just use the search feature. Double click on Terminal, and a black box will appear.

Mac OS X comes with a large set of basic command line tools. However, some tools for examples later in this book aren't present and others are out of date. To install them, you'll need a package manager called Homebrew, which you'll install by entering the commands below. Don't be intimidated—it's one of the more confusing things you'll see in this book. From the Terminal window you just opened, type

1. `xcode-select --install`
2. `ruby -e "$(curl -fsSL https://raw.githubuser content.com/Homebrew/install/master/install)"`
3. `brew install coreutils`
4. `brew install gnu-sed --with-default-names`
5. `brew install grep --with-default-names`
6. `brew install gawk`
7. `brew install bash`

Provide your password when prompted. This will install Homebrew so you can use the `brew` command to perform tasks that appear later in the book without typing the `sudo` command and your password in the future.

Windows

The process is initially more complicated because the environment natively supports two types of command lines that work very differently. The regular command prompt with Windows (which you'll sometimes hear people call a "DOS prompt" because its command structure evolved from the text-based operating system that preceded Windows) is peculiar to that environment.

For this book, you need a `linux` command line—the commands you type in there will also work on Apple and Linux computers. Most Windows users have no use for the `linux` command line, so you'll have to enable a Windows feature to use it. Fortunately, you only need to perform the process outlined below once.

For Windows 10 or Later

1. Search for "Turn Windows features on or off." Alternatively, navigate to Control Panel—Programs and Features—Turn Windows features on or off.
2. Check "Enable Windows Subsystem for Linux."
3. In a web browser, go to https://aka.ms/wslstore.
4. Select the distribution. Ubuntu is recommended.
5. Then click "Get."
6. Create a user name and password. *This user name and password is not connected to your regular Windows password.* You will only use it when interacting with Linux.

7. To simplify work later, we'll make it easy to interact with your Desktop files. Go to Windows Explorer, right click on Properties, and then on the location tab. This will tell you where your desktop is located as shown in figure 1.1.

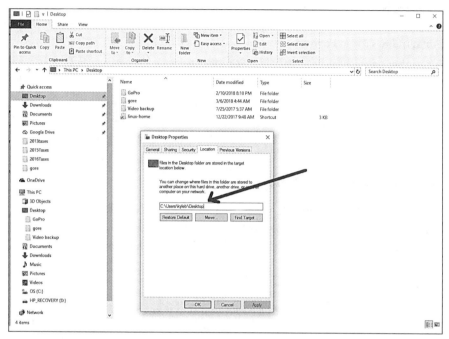

Figure 1.1: **Identifying the filepath for Windows Desktop**

In your command box, type in:

```
ln -s /mnt/c/Users/[YourUserName]/Desktop Desktop
```

The `ln` command creates a link to your normal desktop so you can access your regular desktop through the command line at any time. Notice that the slashes in the filepath are forward rather than backward and that the location you're linking to is that exact same path under `/mnt/c`. You can access any file on your C: drive under `/mnt/c` and any other drive under `/mnt/[DriveLetter]`.

Your system is now ready, but it still needs to be updated. Type the following commands in sequence:

```
sudo apt-get update
sudo apt-get upgrade
```

When asked for your password, use the one you just created when asked. The commands above will take a while because many updates will be installed.

`apt-get update` updates the list of available packages and their versions, but it does not install or upgrade any packages. `apt-get upgrade` actually installs newer versions of the packages you have. After updating the lists, the package manager has information about available updates for the software you have installed

For Windows 8 and Earlier

A number of options are available. For most people, VirtualBox (a free system that provides a virtual Linux environment) is the best option to use with the examples in this book. Many websites (e.g., https://linus.nci.nih.gov/bdge/installUbuntu.html) describe how to do install VirtualBox. Once you've installed VirtualBox, use the interface to find a command prompt.

Meet the Command Line

If you're looking at the black box with a command prompt for the first time, you're probably wondering now what? To get started, here are some commands you'll use in this chapter. First a brief description of the syntax of commands. There are three parts:

1. **Command**—The program or function being used.

   Here is an example of a command that lists the contents of directory sorted alphabetically:

   ```
   ls
   ```

2. **Options**—Parameters (also known as switches) that tell the command how to behave or tell the command to expect certain kinds of information to follow. Options are not usually required but are frequently used.

   Below, the `-t` option is used to list contents of the directory sorted by time stamp:

   ```
   ls -t
   ```

3. **Arguments**—Information passed to the command to process or modify its behavior.

   Below, the directory called `log` is passed as an argument along with the `-t` option to produce a list of the contents of the `log` directory sorted by time stamp:

   ```
   ls -t log
   ```

In this chapter, we will use the following commands:

- **cat (concatentate)**—Create and view files and redirects output to new files.
- **cd (change directory)**—Change the active working directory. If you don't specify which directory you're changing to, you change to the home directory when you first log in. The `cd` command is analogous to double clicking on a folder icon.
- **cp (copy)**—Copy files and directories. Use `cp -R` to copy directories. The `cp` command is analogous to Control-Drag in Windows or Option-Drag in Mac OS where a new copy appears in the new location, but a copy remains in the old location.
- **cut** —Extract fields from delimited files.
- **grep (global regular expression print)**—Helps you to find which parts of files match sophisticated patterns in text files and the output of other commands and which parts don't, `grep` is easily one of the most useful general-purpose data wrangling tools.
- **less** —View files of any size without opening them. Allows paging and searching backwards as well as forward movement through the file.
- **ls (list)**—List files and directories. `ls -l` gives you a long listing that shows properties of files and directories, such as when they were created, how big they are, and what permissions are assigned.
- **pwd (print working directory)**—Print the current working directory. In text-based environments, it's easy to forget where you are. This command tells you the answer.
- **wc (word count)**—Count the number of characters, words, and lines in a file.

At the command prompt, type

```
ls
```

If you're using a Mac, you'll see a number of directories and files. If you're on a Windows computer, you won't see much of anything.

Whether you are on Mac or Windows, type

```
cd Desktop
ls
pwd
```

You can now see all the files and folders on your desktop as well as where you are in the directory hierarchy as displayed in figure 1.2. Now we're starting to get somewhere!

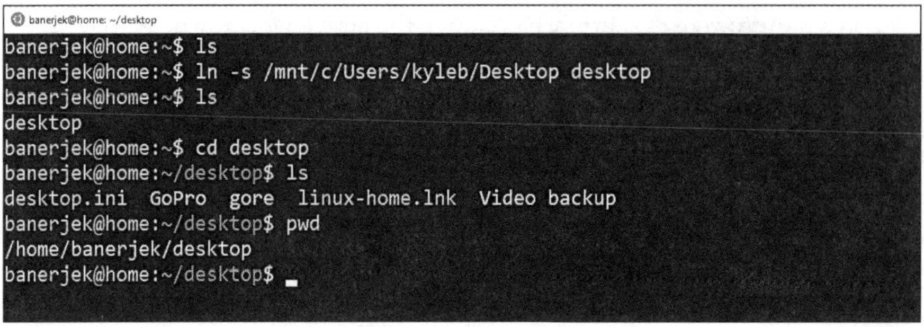

```
banerjek@home: ~/desktop
banerjek@home:~$ ls
banerjek@home:~$ ln -s /mnt/c/Users/kyleb/Desktop desktop
banerjek@home:~$ ls
desktop
banerjek@home:~$ cd desktop
banerjek@home:~/desktop$ ls
desktop.ini  GoPro  gore  linux-home.lnk  Video backup
banerjek@home:~/desktop$ pwd
/home/banerjek/desktop
banerjek@home:~/desktop$
```

Figure 1.2: **Linking to and displaying the contents of a directory**

## CHAPTER 2

Command Line Concepts

The power of the command line comes from its ability to easily direct output of programs into other programs and files. Commands can be thought of as words; as each word has a different meaning, each command performs a different function. Just as words can be combined to create sentences that express an infinite number of ideas, commands can also be combined to perform an infinite number of tasks.

Data analysis and manipulation were some of the first tasks people wanted to perform with computers. As early as the beginning of the 1970s, systems designers devised commands that could efficiently analyze and manipulate data using a computer with a 1-megahertz processor, a few kilobytes of memory, and a slow tape drive. These commands are very powerful and have not changed in decades, and they deliver blistering speed on modern hardware.

If you work on a system migration or have to analyze data in your integrated library system or other major system, you'll work with files containing hundreds of thousands, if not millions, of lines. With the command line, literally a few words on a single line can perform complex tasks on these giant files in a few seconds or less that would be impossible or extremely clunky in a graphical environment.

Two Powerful Symbols

When working with the command line, some characters have special meaning. Typically they are:

```
! # $ ^ & * ? [ ] ( ) { } < > ~ ; ' " \ |
```

Let's start with just two of these special characters: greater than (>) and pipe (|).

Being able to direct the output of programs into other programs and files allows you to assemble small programs in powerful combinations to solve a wide variety of problems. Rather than having to determine program logic, you simply break down what you need into a series of tasks, each of which is handled by a separate program.

Direct Output to a File (Greater than Symbol)

The greater than symbol directs the output of a program to a file. This creates a new file if one doesn't already exist. If the file already exists, it replaces the existing contents. To append to a file rather than replace it, use two greater than symbols (>>).

To understand how this works, we'll use the `cat` command to create a file. Type the following into your command window:

```
cat > mytest.txt
```

When you get a cursor, enter the table below into the window, separating the first and last names with a space and the other elements with a tab.

Lname3, Fname3	Title4	2001
Lname5, Fname5	Title7	2004
Lname6, Fname6	Title2	1999
Lname2, Fname2	Title3	2000
Lname4, Fname4	Title6	2003
Lname1, Fname1	Title8	2005
Lname1, Fname1	Title1	1998
Lname3, Fname3	Title5	2002
Lname4, Fname4	Title9	2009

After entering the last line, type CONTROL+D (hold control key down and type "d").

Now type

```
cat mytest.txt
```

The whole file will flash by the screen very quickly—the `cat` command is useful for creating and typing files. You can use the `rm` command to delete files you no longer need.

Now let's append to the file. Type

```
cat >> mytest.txt
[ENTER]
Lname4, Fname4   Title9 2005
[ENTER]
```

With the name elements separated by spaces and all other elements separated by tabs as before hit CONTROL+D again. Then type

```
cat mytest.txt
```

to verify that the line you typed was added, as demonstrated by figure 2.1.

```
banerjek@BICB242:~/Desktop$ cat > mytest.txt
Lname3, Fname3  Title4  2001
Lname5, Fname5  Title7  2004
Lname6, Fname6  Title2  1999
Lname2, Fname2  Title3  2000
Lname4, Fname4  Title6  2003
Lname1, Fname1  Title8  2005
Lname1, Fname1  Title1  1998
Lname3, Fname3  Title5  2002
Lname4, Fname4  Title9  2009
banerjek@BICB242:~/Desktop$ cat mytest.txt
Lname3, Fname3  Title4  2001
Lname5, Fname5  Title7  2004
Lname6, Fname6  Title2  1999
Lname2, Fname2  Title3  2000
Lname4, Fname4  Title6  2003
Lname1, Fname1  Title8  2005
Lname1, Fname1  Title1  1998
Lname3, Fname3  Title5  2002
Lname4, Fname4  Title9  2009
banerjek@BICB242:~/Desktop$ cat >> mytest.txt
Lname4, Fname4  Title9  2005
banerjek@BICB242:~/Desktop$ cat mytest.txt
Lname3, Fname3  Title4  2001
Lname5, Fname5  Title7  2004
Lname6, Fname6  Title2  1999
Lname2, Fname2  Title3  2000
Lname4, Fname4  Title6  2003
Lname1, Fname1  Title8  2005
Lname1, Fname1  Title1  1998
Lname3, Fname3  Title5  2002
Lname4, Fname4  Title9  2009
Lname4, Fname4  Title9  2005
banerjek@BICB242:~/Desktop$ _
```

Figure 2.1: **Using** `cat` **to create, display, and append to a file**

Direct Output to Another Program (Pipe Symbol)

You'll often find yourself needing to direct the output of one program to another. For example, you might want to count, sort, and select only some of the output to form a program. The pipe (|) symbol allows you to combine as many programs as you want. Let's learn a couple more commands. The `cut` command is very useful for extracting columns from a delimited file, the `grep` command is useful for finding lines that contain what you're interested in, and `wc` is useful for counting words, lines, and characters.

If you type in:

```
cat mytest.txt | cut -f 1,3
```

you'll get the first and third columns. You can connect as many pipes as you want. For example, if you want the first and third columns for the entries associated with author 4, you can pipe the above command into `grep`, which will search each line for entries containing name4.

```
cat mytest.txt | cut -f 1,3 | grep "name4"
```

If you wanted to count the number of entries associated with `name4`, you can pipe that output into the `wc` command, count the lines, and see that author 4 wrote three books.

```
cat mytest.txt | cut -f 1,3 | grep "name4" | wc -l
```

You can string as many pipe symbols as you want together (see figure 2.2).

```
banerjek@BICB242:~/Desktop$ cat mytest.txt | cut -f 1,3
Lname3,  Fname3   2001
Lname5,  Fname5   2004
Lname6,  Fname6   1999
Lname2,  Fname2   2000
Lname4,  Fname4   2003
Lname1,  Fname1   2005
Lname1,  Fname1   1998
Lname3,  Fname3   2002
Lname4,  Fname4   2009
Lname4,  Fname4   2005
banerjek@BICB242:~/Desktop$ cat mytest.txt | cut -f 1,3 | grep "name4"
Lname4,  Fname4   2003
Lname4,  Fname4   2009
Lname4,  Fname4   2005
banerjek@BICB242:~/Desktop$ cat mytest.txt | cut -f 1,3 |grep "name4" |wc -l
3
banerjek@BICB242:~/Desktop$ cat mytest.txt | cut -f 1,3 |grep "name4" > name4.txt
banerjek@BICB242:~/Desktop$ cat name4.txt
Lname4,  Fname4   2003
Lname4,  Fname4   2009
Lname4,  Fname4   2005
banerjek@BICB242:~/Desktop$ _
```

Figure 2.2: **Using pipes to chain commands and sending the output to the screen or a file**

Command Substitution

In addition to being able to direct the output of commands to files and other commands, you'll sometimes need to use them as arguments to another command. An argument is simply information used by a command as input. For example, when you typed `cat mytest.txt`, mytest.txt is an argument for the `cat` command. For practical purposes, command substitution serves a similar function to pipes—to allow you to use the output of one command as the input for another. In many cases, either pipes or command substitution can be used interchangeably. However, command substitution allows you to do things that would not be possible with pipes. In figure 2.3, the `echo` command, which is normally used to print text to the screen or a file, is used to display the output of the `date` command interspersed with text.

```
echo "The date command can be used to display dates in
    most formats. For example, three weeks from now is
    $(date --date '3 weeks' +'%A, %B %d'). It can also
    be used to normalize dates such as $(date -d 'march
    8, 2018' +'%Y-%m-%d')"
```

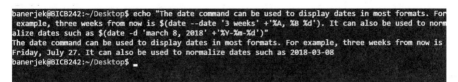

Figure 2.3: **Command substitution example**

Notice how the `date` command is used twice within the `echo` command to do different things. When you're working with library data, you'll use pipes more often than the command substitution, but command substitution allows you to perform more complex tasks than you could perform with pipes alone. Command substitution is frequently useful for performing tasks such as running a process on every file in a directory that meets certain criteria.

In the figure 2.3 example, the `date` command is used to express a date in the future, which is be useful for tasks such as setting embargo periods and for interpreting and converting a textual date representation to a computer friendly format. Although the use of the `date` command here is trivial, it is very handy for reformatting and normalizing dates in library data. The important thing to remember is not how to use the `date` command, but rather that whenever it's necessary to perform a task that a lot of people will perform, it's a good idea to see if a command that does what you need already exists—because often it will.

Sometimes you'll want to use each line of output from a command to be used as a series of inputs for a program. When you need to do that, the `xargs` utility is helpful. `xargs` can sometimes be used interchangeably with the syntax listed above. For example,

```
ls *.txt | xargs rm
```

and

```
rm $(ls *.txt)
```

are equivalent. In this particular case,

```
rm *.txt
```

would also work, but as you learn more sophisticated commands, you'll find this functionality very useful.

In a data wrangling context, `xargs` is particularly useful for performing an operation on a list of files created by another program. For example,

```
find . -type f | xargs sed -i 's/search_for/replace_
    with'
```

Locates all files in a directory hierarchy and replaces every occurrence of `"search_for"` with `"replace_with."` Later in the book, you'll learn how to use the `find` and `sed` commands as well as see examples where `xargs` is used.

Regular Expressions—The Swiss Army Knife for Data

Few concepts are more useful than regular expressions. Regular expressions are special strings that allow search and replace based on patterns, and they are supported on all operating systems. A single regular expression can perform tasks such as:

- using logic, capitalization, edges of words/lines, express ranges, use bits (or all) of what you matched in replacements
- converting free or delimited text into XML and other formats, codes, and vice versa
- finding complex patterns spread over multiple lines using proximity indicators
- selecting and modifying specific text you're interested in

Regular expressions can be confusing at first, but they're easy and very handy once you get the hang of them. The good news is that if you have problems constructing or understanding one, all you need to do is find a programmer. All programmers know regular expressions and can probably tell you what to do in less than a few minutes. Regular expression support is built into most of the commands useful for data analysis, and it can even be found in desktop software such as Microsoft Word.

It's important to be aware that regular expression support differs across applications and platforms. Generally speaking, these differences apply to more sophisticated regular expressions. This book focuses on basic functionality that is more universally supported, but it will also give you ideas for what kinds of problems regular expressions can solve.

Be aware that regular expressions:

- are case sensitive unless you specify otherwise
- only match the first occurrence unless you specify otherwise

- are "greedy" and will match as much as they can. For example, a wildcard that matches any character will match to the end of the input, not just to the end of a word.
- assign special meaning to many punctuation symbols. To match a punctuation symbol, you need to "escape" it to tell the program you're looking for that symbol and that you don't want it interpreted as it normally would be.
- are incredibly powerful and can do many things not covered in this chapter, which focuses on addressing common needs in library work. Those seeking more information should consult one of the many books about regular expressions. There are many websites (e.g., see the tutorial at https://www.regular-expressions.info/) that can help you learn more about regular expressions.

When you first start working with regular expressions, the syntax can be daunting. Don't try to learn too much too fast. Rather, learn or look things up in the moment and you'll be an expert before you know it!

To help you learn regular expressions, we're going to experiment with grep, which you used in the section introducing you to pipes. If you're using a Mac, your version of grep is out of date. If you haven't already, type

```
brew install grep --with-default-names
```

at the command line. This step is unnecessary for Windows users.

Before we begin, let's add another few lines to our test file. As before, put tabs between the names and titles and between the titles and dates. Notice that the capitalization and the formatting of the names and dates is not consistent with the other entries.

```
cat >> mytest.txt
Fname4 Lname4    Title10      c2005
fname6 lname6    title11      2010-12-01
lname6, fname6        tITLE12      7/13/1967
Fname7 lname7    title14      2000-04
[CONTROL+D]
```

Literal Characters

The most basic form of matching is one or more specific characters. When you typed in

```
grep "name4"
```

name4 is what is called a "string literal." This is very similar to looking for something using the "find" feature in a word processor, except a string literal is case sensitive and the find feature normally is not.

Special Characters

Regular expressions are powerful because they provide special characters that allow you to match complex patterns. Learning these patterns can be confusing, so only the most commonly used patterns are introduced in this chapter.

Wildcard Characters

Many punctuation symbols have special meaning in the context of regular expressions

- . (dot)—matches any single character
- ? (question mark)—matches zero or one of the preceding character
- * (asterisk)—matches zero or more of the preceding character
- + (plus sign)—matches one or more of the preceding character
- \ (backslash)—used to indicate the next character receives special handling. Special characters following a backslash are interpreted as string literals and the backslash is used to type special characters. For example, \n indicates a newline and \t indicates a tab.

Figure 2.4 shows examples of the dot, asterisk, and plus sign used in our file. Notice what is and what is not matched. Notice also that the plus and question marks were preceded by a backslash—something that was necessary for matching in this particular implementation of grep. Regular expression support differs, so when something doesn't seem to work, experimenting with syntax can help.

Often you need to match the beginning or end of a line or multiple character variations. Regular expressions make this easy.

- ^ (caret)—matches the beginning of a line. When used within brackets, it negates the search, which means it will match anything except what appears between the brackets
- $ (dollar sign)—matches the end of a line
- [ ] (brackets)—used to express a range of characters
- - (hyphen)—used to express ranges

Figure 2.5 demonstrates the basic operation of these characters. In the first example, all lines beginning with "l" (el) are found. The second example selects lines that end with "9." The third identifies all titles that don't begin with a capital letter. The third example is more complicated in the following ways:

1. We invoke the P switch for Perl regular expressions so that we can type special characters using a backslash and easily readable letter

rather than typing it in. In this case, we use `\t` to represent the tab character.

2. Regular expression matches are greedy because they match the longest group of characters possible, so finding the title field means we search from the beginning of the line. This is starting to look complicated, but it really isn't if you think about it one component at a time.

```
grep -P "^[^\t]*\t[a-z]" mytest.txt
```

```
banerjek@BICB242:~/Desktop$ grep "itle1" mytest.txt
Lname1, Fname1  Title1  1998
Fname4 Lname4    Title10 c2005
fname6 lname6    title11 2010-12-01
Fname7 lname7    title14 2000-04
banerjek@BICB242:~/Desktop$ grep ".04" mytest.txt
Lname5, Fname5  Title7  2004
Fname7 lname7    title14 2000-04
banerjek@BICB242:~/Desktop$ grep "19\?" mytest.txt
Lname3, Fname3  Title4  2001
Lname6, Fname6  Title2  1999
Lname1, Fname1  Title8  2005
Lname1, Fname1  Title1  1998
Fname4 Lname4    Title10 c2005
fname6 lname6    title11 2010-12-01
lname6, fname6  tITLE12 7/13/1967
Fname7 lname7    title14 2000-04
banerjek@BICB242:~/Desktop$ grep "19*" mytest.txt
Lname3, Fname3  Title4  2001
Lname6, Fname6  Title2  1999
Lname1, Fname1  Title8  2005
Lname1, Fname1  Title1  1998
Fname4 Lname4    Title10 c2005
fname6 lname6    title11 2010-12-01
lname6, fname6  tITLE12 7/13/1967
Fname7 lname7    title14 2000-04
banerjek@BICB242:~/Desktop$ grep "19\+" mytest.txt
Lname6, Fname6  Title2  1999
Lname1, Fname1  Title1  1998
lname6, fname6  tITLE12 7/13/1967
banerjek@BICB242:~/Desktop$
```

Figure 2.4: **Experimenting with regular expressions**

```
banerjek@BICB242:~/Desktop$ grep "^l" mytest.txt
lname6, fname6  tITLE12 7/13/1967
banerjek@BICB242:~/Desktop$ grep "9$" mytest.txt
Lname6, Fname6  Title2  1999
Lname4, Fname4  Title9  2009
banerjek@BICB242:~/Desktop$ grep -P "^[^\t]*\t[a-z]" mytest.txt
fname6 lname6    title11 2010-12-01
lname6, fname6  tITLE12 7/13/1967
Fname7 lname7    title14 2000-04
banerjek@BICB242:~/Desktop$
```

Figure 2.5: **Capturing beginnings and ends of lines as well as ranges of character**

In real world scenarios, you're often looking for things that don't follow a pattern. Fortunately, grep has an option—namely the -v switch that tells grep to select only those lines that don't match what we're searching for. For example, if we expect the first field to contain a capitalized last name followed by a comma, followed by a space, followed by a capitalized first name, we can find them easily with

```
grep -v "^[A-Z][a-z]*[0-9], [A-Z][a-z]*[0-9]" mytest.txt
```

Notice that after the lower case letters in the name, we look for a digit. That would normally not be necessary, except these names end with digits.

If we want to make sure all the dates in the last field are a four-digit year in the twentieth or twenty-first century, the expression becomes

```
grep -vP "\t[12][0-9][0-9][0-9]$" mytest.txt
```

because we know the year must begin with a "1" or "2" and be followed by digits. Again, we've used the -P option so we could type the tab as \t rather than typing the tab key directly (see figure 2.6).

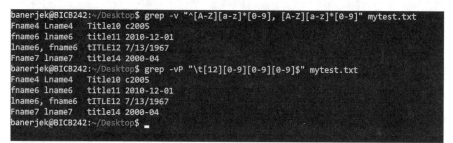

Figure 2.6: **Negative regular expression matches**

If you're wondering if the regular expression could be modified to identify dates that aren't valid because they occur in the future, the answer is they can. However, that requires learning a few more symbols and the syntax is more complex. Likewise, the expression that identifies improperly formatted names could be modified to deal with middle names, suffixes, and prefixes. However, that would be difficult for someone who is just learning regular expressions to decipher. Most of the problems you'll encounter in daily work aren't so complex.

Be aware that the -v switch is peculiar to grep. However, other regular expression tools have their own ways of doing negative searches.

If your file contains diacritics, you may get an error such as "binary file matches" when you use grep. If this happens, use grep -a —this tells grep to treat the file as plain text.

Logical Operators

As powerful as wild cards, ranges, and bracketed expressions are, you sometimes need logical operators such as AND and OR to express what you're looking for.

Using AND with `grep` is incredibly easy. Remember how you used pipes to direct the output of one command into another? With `grep`, the AND function is achieved by piping the output through a second `grep` command. For example, if you wanted all works by author Lname4 written in 2009, you could simply type

```
grep "Lname4" mytest.txt | grep "2009"
```

In other non-grep contexts, the ampersand (&) is often used to express logical AND. In practice, knowledge of the order of information in lines delivers this functionality.

On the other hand, logical OR is a useful operator that can be expressed with "|" (pipe). For example,

```
grep "Lname3\|2005" mytest.txt
```

yields the results in figure 2.7.

Figure 2.7: **Performing AND and OR searches with** `grep`

Although that example might not seem particularly useful, the value of the OR operator becomes more apparent with more complex patterns.

Grouping

By creating groups within patterns you are matching, you can do things such as extract specific information from larger matches, matching something that has matched a previously matched group, and perform substitutions.

Sounds clear as mud, doesn't it? The idea is simple—you can use parentheses to break portions of your match into groups. Just as you used brackets in figure 2.5 to express a range of characters, you can use parentheses to express a sequential pattern that can contain virtually anything, including other groups.

An easier way to understand grouping is by example. For this, we're going to introduce a new command:

```
sed (stream editor)
```

sed allows you to easily perform complex manipulations on very large files and is one of the most important tools used to modify data. There are many ways to use sed but the most common way takes the form

```
cat mytest.txt | sed 's/searchtext/replacetext/g'
```

If you have a Mac, its version of sed may be out of date. You can update it by typing:

```
brew install gnu-sed --with-default-names
```

if you haven't already. Windows users do not need to perform this step.

The above command types the file mytest.txt to the screen while replacing all instances of searchtext with replacetext. The "g" at the end indicates that the replacement is global—otherwise, sed only replaces the first occurrence it finds on each line.

For a simple example, first type out the file with the cat command as shown in figure 2.8. Notice how a few of the names are not in inverted order. The good news is that with regular expression grouping, you can use sed to fix this in seconds.

```
banerjek@BICB242: ~/Desktop
banerjek@BICB242:~/Desktop$ cat mytest.txt
Lname3, Fname3  Title4   2001
Lname5, Fname5  Title7   2004
Lname6, Fname6  Title2   1999
Lname2, Fname2  Title3   2000
Lname4, Fname4  Title6   2003
Lname1, Fname1  Title8   2005
Lname1, Fname1  Title1   1998
Lname3, Fname3  Title5   2002
Lname4, Fname4  Title9   2009
Lname4, Fname4  Title9   2005
Fname4 Lname4   Title10  c2005
fname6 lname6   title11  2010-12-01
lname6, fname6  tITLE12  7/13/1967
Fname7 lname7   title14  2000-04
banerjek@BICB242:~/Desktop$ cat mytest.txt |sed 's/^\([a-zA-Z0-9]*\) \([^\t]*\)/\2, \1/'
Lname3, Fname3  Title4   2001
Lname5, Fname5  Title7   2004
Lname6, Fname6  Title2   1999
Lname2, Fname2  Title3   2000
Lname4, Fname4  Title6   2003
Lname1, Fname1  Title8   2005
Lname1, Fname1  Title1   1998
Lname3, Fname3  Title5   2002
Lname4, Fname4  Title9   2009
Lname4, Fname4  Title9   2005
Lname4, Fname4  Title10  c2005
lname6, fname6  title11  2010-12-01
lname6, fname6  tITLE12  7/13/1967
lname7, Fname7  title14  2000-04
banerjek@BICB242:~/Desktop$
```

Figure 2.8: **Fixing misordered names with** sed

Don't worry if your eyeballs turned inside out when you saw the expression—it's really much simpler than it looks. Table 2.1 describes what is happening.

Table 2-1: **Analysis of expression to change names from direct order to indirect order**

`cat mytest.txt |sed 's/^\([a-zA-Z0-9 \.\-]*\) \([^\t]*\)/\2, \1/'`

`cat mytest .txt	sed 's`	Sends mytest.txt to the screen and to the sed program which replaces the first and second expressions following the "s" which are delimited by forward slashes
`^`	Start capture at beginning of line
`\(`	Store everything between \(and \) in \1
`[a-zA-Z0-9 \.\-]*`	Zero or more letters, numbers, periods or hyphens. The space captures middle names
`[space] following \)`	A space following everything stored in \1
`\([^\t]*\)`	Zero or more of any character except a tab (because the tab indicates the beginning of the next field, store in \2
`/\2, \1/`	Replace the previous expression followed by field 2, a comma, a space, and then the first field—effectively putting the last name first, a comma, and then the first name

Regular syntax is confusing at first, but it's easy once you get used to it. There are many special types of regular expressions that aren't discussed in this book. However, table 2.2 shows a small number of expressions that can be used to solve almost any problem.

Table 2-2: **Regular expression cheat sheet**

`^`	Match start of the line
`$`	Match end of the line
`.`	Match any single character
`*`	Match zero or more of the previous character
	Match zero or more of ABCDGHIJ012345
`[^A-C]`	Match any one character that is NOT A,B, or C
`(dog)`	Match the word "dog", including case, and remember that text to be used later in the match or replacement
`\1`	Insert the first remembered text as if it were typed here (\2 for second, \3 for 3rd, etc.)

(continued)

Table 2-2: **Regular expression cheat sheet** *(cont'd)*

\	Use to match special characters or convert what is normally a special character to a regular character. For example, \w indicates a word character, \n indicates a newline, but \\ matches a backslash and * matches an asterisk.

When the expressions in table 2.2 aren't enough, explore online because there is probably a way to solve the problem. For example, the capitalization for both titles and names is wrong and the dates are all inconsistent. If you want to fix that, it's very possible to do so in a single line as figure 2.9 demonstrates.

Figure 2.9: **Fixing multiple problems in one line**

This looks hopelessly confusing if you're new to regular expressions, but the important things to know are that:

- You can do amazing things in a single line.
- Different regular expressions can legitimately be used to perform the same task.
- It's easiest to look up the information yourself or ask for help when you need to learn more.

- You can break complicated regular expressions into a series of much simpler ones.
- Programs and utilities implement regular expressions differently, so some that work in one environment won't work in another. This means trial and error is sometimes necessary to get them to work.

> Both sed and grep process data one line at a time. As a result, neither "sees" newline characters even though both make it easy to match the end of a line.
>
> This means that if you need to match an expression that includes a new-line character—namely any multiline expression—you should either replace the newline characters using the tr command and then change them back in a separate step later. Chapter 5 contains more information on how to do this.

Scripting

Scripts are simple text files that allow you to combine utilities and program written in any language—or multiple languages, for that matter. Scripts are great for automating processing. If you're wondering how scripting differs from programing, scripting is typically written in a high-level language for limited use cases, whereas programming usually involves writing instructions in a single language that will be compiled into machine code for long-term use. Over time, the distinction between scripting and programming has blurred, and it's not important for our purposes here.

For example, the one-line fix in figure 2.9 is confusing. Also, you might not want to type it out every time. Using a text editor or cat, create a file named myscript containing the following, as demonstrated in figure 2.10:

```
cat mytest.txt |sed 's/^\([a-zA-Z0-9]*\) \([^\t]*\)/\2,
    \1/' > names_fixed
cat names_fixed | sed 's/[^ \t]\+/\L\u&/g' > capitalization
    _fixed
cat capitalization_fixed |sed 's/[^\t]*\([12][0-9][0-9]
    [0-9]\)[^\t]*$/\1/' > dates_fixed
cat dates_fixed
```

```
banerjek@BICB242:~/Desktop$ cat > myscript
cat mytest.txt |sed 's/^\([a-zA-Z0-9]*\) \([^\t]*\)/\2, \1/' > names_fixed
cat names_fixed | sed 's/[^ \t]\+/\L\u&/g' > capitalization_fixed
cat capitalization_fixed |sed 's/[^\t]*\([12][0-9][0-9][0-9]\)[^\t]*$/\1/' > dates_fixed
cat dates_fixed
banerjek@BICB242:~/Desktop$ chmod 700 myscript
banerjek@BICB242:~/Desktop$ ./myscript
Lname3, Fname3  Title4  2001
Lname5, Fname5  Title7  2004
Lname6, Fname6  Title2  1999
Lname2, Fname2  Title3  2000
Lname4, Fname4  Title6  2003
Lname1, Fname1  Title8  2005
Lname1, Fname1  Title1  1998
Lname3, Fname3  Title5  2002
Lname4, Fname4  Title9  2009
Lname4, Fname4  Title9  2005
Lname4, Fname4  Title10 2005
Lname6, Fname6  Title11 2010
Lname6, Fname6  Title12 1967
Lname7, Fname7  Title14 2000
banerjek@BICB242:~/Desktop$ _
```

Figure 2.10: **Creating and running a script**

Then type

```
chmod 700 myscript
```

to make it so you can run the file like a program. Then type

```
./myscript
```

to run it. By modifying the myscript file, you can make it do virtually anything. With a simple text editor—you can use any editor that allows you to save files in plain text—you can write sets of instructions that perform incredibly complex tasks that call many different programs.

Scripts allow you to create custom commands that allow you to automate any process you'll need to use again. Scripts also allow you to simplify processes by breaking them into separate steps that can be easily modified. Although you can learn to write useful scripts in less than two minutes, you'll want to know how to do more if you regularly perform any serious data wrangling. Being able to execute a sequence of commands is very useful. However, you'll eventually want scripts that can accept input that changes, decide what to do based on criteria you specify, and loop through files, file systems, and online services to perform repetitive tasks. Don't worry about that for now. This topic will be covered in chapter 8.

As you work through the code examples in this book, be aware that some single line examples may wrap.

## CHAPTER 3

Understanding Formats

David Forero

A lthough formats may seem technical, most of the time they simply describe how text is ordered—meaning you can use a wide variety of simple tools to work with almost any format. When you hear people mention HTML, XML, RDF, JSON, Linked Data, and a number of other formats, they are often talking about textual data that you could read and modify using any word processor.

Text is one of the most common ways of storing and exchanging information. This chapter discusses ways of structuring and encoding textual information. We also discuss some of the more common formats, what they are good for, and their pitfalls.

To understand formats, it's necessary to familiarize yourself with some jargon. The first is "text." Most English speakers define "text" as the fifty-two letters of the alphabet (both upper and lower case) plus ten digits, and maybe the thirty or so weird punctuation marks they've seen on keyboards. For computers, there are specific encoding standards. These standards associate specific characters (including non-printable characters like spaces) with binary values. For example, in a common encoding called ASCII (American Standard Code for Information Interchange), the letter A is equal to 01101101 (or 109). The international standard today is UTF (Unicode Transformation Format). Although UTF is the current standard, many tools and documents were created before its invention. Consequently, there are still a considerable number of tools and documents that don't use UTF. ASCII was the most common standard before UTF; because UTF was designed to make the transition, all values for ASCII characters are the same in UTF. UTF is just a lot bigger. Where ASCII originally had 128 and expanded to 256 characters (Extended ASCII), UTF can

David Forero has more than two decades of experience helping people solve problems using technology in environments including higher education, K–12, nonprofit, Fortune 500, and a tech startup. In 2015, he completed an MLIS and is now the technology director for the Library at OHSU.

support over a million characters (although it currently has only 140,000 unique characters). The larger number of characters was needed to accommodate non-Latin-based languages.

Once you have defined text, you can work on what to do with it. There are two aspects to formatting text. The first is structure. Structure is as simple as the order of the text. A simple example would be a list of books and their author.

The Vegetarian	Han Kang
A Horse Walks into a Bar	David Grossman
Flights	Olga Tokarczuk

Not all the authors have the same number of names, even though everyone in this example does. The classic way to make it clear which name is a first, middle, or last name is to insert blanks for the nonexistent information. We have then created the next level of complexity of structure, the table.

Title	Given Name	Family Name
The Vegetarian	Kang	Han
A Horse Walks into a Bar	David	Grossman
Flights	Olga	Tokarczuk

Here a table is displayed graphically to help people read it but, a table is not very readable by a computer. Typically, some character or characters are inserted between data items to create the columns of a table. For example, inserting commas between data items would result in something like this:

```
Title,Given Name,Family Name
The Vegetarian,Kang,Han
A Horse Walks into a Bar,David,Grossman
Flights,Olga,Tokarczuk
```

This is not necessarily very pretty, but it is very readable by computers. This encoding of this structure is so common it has a specific name: Comma Separated Values (CSV). There are other encodings that are very similar. Replacing the commas with the non-printable tab character is equally machine-readable and slightly more attractive for humans to read. Essentially, you can delimit the data with any character (or string of characters) as long as that character is not part of the original data.

Another way to deal with the problem would be to mark the data itself. Anyone who uses the World Wide Web uses Hyper-Text Markup Language (HTML) to specify how their web browser reads information. HTML tags data. For example, you can recreate the above table like this (see figure 3.1):

```
<html>
    <body>
        <table>
            <tr>
                <td>The Vegetarian</td>
                <td>Kang</td>
                <td>Han</td>
            </tr>
            <tr>
                <td>A Horse Walks Into a Bar</td>
                <td>David</td>
                <td>Grossman</td>
            </tr>
            <tr>
                <td>Flights</td>
                <td>Olga</td>
                <td>Tokarczuk</td>
            </tr>
        </table>
    </body>
</html>
```

Figure 3.1: **HTML example**

HTML is hierarchical, meaning each tag must be nested within another tag. The overall HTML document contains a body element, which is the main display entity for HTML. Inside the body element, a table object contains multiple `tr` (table row) elements. Each table row contains multiple `td` (table data) elements that contain the data to be displayed.

You may notice that this information has become bulkier in terms of the total number of characters required to convey the same information. Our original simple text example contained only 86 characters but encoding it in HTML expanded the size to 428 characters. Increasing the size of the data more than fourfold while making it more difficult for humans to read may seem like a high price. However, there are benefits that outweigh those costs, including greater flexibility in systematically rendering the table on a web page.

HTML is a subset of yet another language known as eXtensible Markup Language (XML). XML is like HTML in that we mark data by surrounding it with a tag. The biggest difference is that HTML defines a limited number of markup tags to facilitate displaying information on the web, whereas XML defines almost nothing. The tags that can be used are specific to each implementation and are defined by a document known as a schema, which states which tags can be used and how they may be constructed.

For example, libraries frequently use Dublin Core—a set of fifteen elements—to describe books. Dublin Core only defines what elements should be stored—Dublin Core metadata can be in any format. However, there is an XML implementation that defines what elements can be stored. For example, the work below is a translation. If we want access points for the original title as well as the translated title and also for the translator, we store the original title in another title field and add the translator as a contributor (see figure 3.2).

```
<?xml version="1.0" encoding="UTF-8"?>
    <metadata
        xmlns:xsi="http://www.w3.org/2001/XMLSchema-instance"
        xmlns:dc="http://purl.org/dc/elements/1.1/">
        <dc:title>Ch'aesikchuŭija. English</dc:title>
        <dc:title>The Vegetarian</dc:title>
        <dc:creator>Kang, Han</dc:creator>
        <dc:contributor>Smith, Deborah, translator</dc:
        contributor>
</metadata>
```

Figure 3.2: **Dublin Core expressed as XML**

As is the case with HTML, we still have a hierarchy, but it's much shallower. Dublin Core defines a few repeatable tags that label the function of the data. You can tell that "The Vegetarian" is a title by its tag rather than its spatial relationship to the other data.

Note that the XML indicates what text encoding is used and specifically references the definitions used for the object—valid XML code assumes very little and is explicitly about *everything*. You'll notice that there is no distinction between the original title and the translated title because simple Dublin Core provides no mechanism to communicate that distinction. Qualified Dublin Core allows you to indicate that it's an alternative title, but if you wanted the exact distinction to preserved, you'd need to use another XML schema.

Your choice of schema is important. You may sometimes have to choose a less expressive schema to maintain compatibility with software and other data. For example, simple Dublin Core is one of the least expressive schemas, but it is also by far the most widely supported. As a result, a great deal of library data is encoded in simple Dublin Core.

JavaScript Object Notation (JSON) is another format that for communicating non-tabular data. As its name implies, this format is often used with JavaScript to allow web pages to better store and query data. JSON is similar to XML in that it provides a structure to define elements, as opposed to defining the elements themselves as is the case with HTML. JSON and XML are better thought of as meta-markup languages than as languages in their own right. Our original data would look like this in JSON (see figure 3.3).

```
{ "metadata": {
    "dc:title": ["Ch'aesikchuŭija","The Vegetarian"],
    "dc:creator": ["Kang, Han"],
    "dc:contributor": [ "Smith, Deborah"]
} }
```

Figure 3.3: **Dublin Core expressed as JSON**

The JSON example is similar to what we saw earlier with XML, but you'll notice that repeated elements are labeled together rather than having individual entries—this will simplify parsing later.

Why do we need both JSON and XML? Briefly, one is often much easier to use than the other. Both can be used for virtually any purpose, but XML is best suited for document markup and JSON is usually better for structured data interchange. JSON is a simpler, less verbose format that interfaces with computer programs more easily.

However, XML makes it easier to communicate mixed content such as formatted text—expressing that a single word within a sentence should be rendered in bold text is awkward in JSON, but very easy in XML and HTML. Moreover, XML allows metadata to be included in the form of attributes within tags, which makes it an excellent choice for some types of complex hierarchical data.

Now that you're familiar with the differences between delimited and marked-up data as well as the implications of different encodings, it's time to talk about structure. We have alluded to some of the structural implications of the different encodings. Delimited data tends to be structured as a table. Markup data can express tables but is normally used to express hierarchical structures. From the HTML example, you can see the structure is a table that has rows nested in it and cells nested within the rows.

Another term that is growing more popular in the library world is Linked Data. Linked Data is not a format like HTML, XML, or JSON. Rather, it's more of a concept of how data should be organized and used. Imagine if your data were encoded in a way so that once it was properly formatted and published, you or others could make structured queries of not only your data but also related data compiled by others.

To accomplish this, you'll want to organize their data so that it can most easily be used. This means you must publish a specification with your data explaining how it is organized so that a computer program can interpret it. Then you'll need to reduce your data to the simplest structure possible. That's what Resource Description Framework (RDF) does, and that simple structure is known as a "triple." A triple is essentially a sentence that contains a single fact about something.

For example, the creator for the object is "Kang, Han" is a triple. This conveys the same information as the JSON in figure 3.3, but in a more basic format known as Turtle (Terse RDF Triple Language), which was specifically developed to express RDF (see figure 3.4).

```
@prefix rdf: <http://www.w3.org/1999/02/22-rdf-syntax-ns#>.
@prefix dc:  <http://purl.org/dc/elements/1.1/>.
<https://doi.org/10.1080/07374836.2018.1437098>
    dc:title "Ch'aesikchuŭija";
    dc:title "The Vegetarian";
    dc:creator: "Kang, Han";
    dc:contributor: "Smith, Deborah".
```

Figure 3.4: **Dublin Core expressed as Linked Data**

This Turtle example is bulky—partly because it's trying to make sure the simplest form of the data is available. This is called a triple. Triples are a statement of a subject, predicate, and an object. For example: Subject: https://doi.org/10.1080/07374836.2018.1437098 has a predicate of: "has a title of" and the object is "The Vegetarian." These triples are then stored in a special type of database known as a "graph database," which is optimized for processing this sort of information.

Understanding how to chain many triples together to make large and complex bodies of data is beyond the scope of this book. However, this linked data approach can be very helpful in taking separate collections of data and trying to ask questions about relationships without restructuring the data.

At this point you should understand that there are many ways of structuring data and that the structure plays a role in determining what you can do with the data. Most of these data formats can be fairly easily understood with a little patience, and you can convert one form to another to serve your needs. Later in the book we will give examples of how to manipulate text to get information out or to transform the text into something more useful for a specific purpose.

Of the formats librarians often work with, MARC (MAchine Readable Cataloging) deserves special mention. MARC is thought of as a format, but in reality, it is three things: 1) a physical format; 2) a set of tags, indicators, and subfields; and 3) the actual data. The physical MARC format is a binary structure originally developed in the 1960s to distribute records on tape. It looks like figure 3.5.

```
04883cam  2200661 i 4500001001300000003000600013005001700
01900800041000360100017000770400016200094020004900256020000
04600305029002100351029002100372029002100393029002100414
03100060043503500210044104200080046205000260047007000260
04960820015005220490009005372450094005462640084006402640
01000724300004500734336002600779337002800805338002700833
52016240086050400510248450506120253565000500314765000230
31976500039032206500044032596500076033036500065033796500
07003444650004903514650002103563650004603584650004503630
65000460367565000500372165000700377165000590384165000640
39006500043039647000029040077000028040367000034040064938-
00290409893800410412793800410416899400120420900cn957134124O-
CoLC20181030121806.0170321t20172017ilua     b    001 0 eng
a   2016056887  aDLCbengerdacDLCdYDXdOCLCOdOCLCQdOCLCFdPSC-
dGZNdKSUdNRCdYDXdTWTdSDSdWAUdZCUdFDAdCHVBKdOCLCOdBDXdNMCdO-
CLCQdIOGdTYCdOCLCQdTXMdCRUdAGL  a9780838915035q(paperback
;qalkaline paper)  a0838915035q(paperback ;qalkaline paper)1
aCHBISb0109510101 aCHDSBb0067342511 aCHVBKb4916326061 aCH-
VBKb494692316  ad   a(OCoLC)957134124  apcc00aZ678.93.I57bM54
20170 aZ678.93.I57bM54 201700a025.04223  aOHSM00aMigrating
library data :ba practical manual /cedited by Kyle Banerjee
and Bonnie Parks. 1aChicago :bNeal-Schuman, an imprint of
the American Library Association,c2017. 4cÃ2017  axix, 251
pages :billustrations ;c26 cm  atextbtxt2rdacontent  aun-
mediatedbn2rdamedia  avolumebnc2rdacarrier  a"Most librar-
ians and staff participate in at least one data migration
during their careers. And since the new systems inevitably
work differently than the old ones and require different
data to function, it's always a challenge to plan smooth
migrations that position libraries to immediately lever-
age new system capabilities. Using step-by-step instruc-
tions and checklists, this book offers expert advice to help
library staff without programming knowledge address common
conceptual and technical issues encountered in migrations.
An important planning and implementation tool that will
```

help prevent headaches and frustration, this book offers:
a holistic view of migrating different types of library
data in ILSes, institutional repositories, DAMs, and other
types of systems used to manage data and operations; shows
how to analyze, clean, and manipulate data using skills and
tools available to most libraries; demonstrates how to work
with specific data types typically encountered such as MARC,
XML, and delimited text; examines issues that affect specific areas such as acquisitions, circulation, licensing, and
institutional repositories; addresses how to handle changes
in authentication management or when moving into a wholly
new environment such as a shared catalog; thoroughly covers testing, the final migration process, and putting the new
system into full production; offers guidance on planning for
system freeze, staff training, and how to deal with fallout; provides step-by-step instructions as well as useful
checklists for 'go live' readiness, post-migration functionality"--cPublisher's website. aIncludes bibliographical
references and index.00tUnderstanding the migration process
/rBonnie Parks --tFormats and data cleaning /rDavid Forero
--tThinking beyond Excel /rKate Hill --tWorking with MARC
data /rTerry Reese --tBibliographic and item data /rKelley
McGrath --tAcquisitions /rSiãon Romaine --tPatron data and
authentication /rNathan Mealey --tSerials /rElan May Rinck
--tElectronic resources management /rTodd Enoch --tInstitu-
tional repositories and digital collections /rKyle Banerjee
--tMigrating to shared systems /rAl Cornish --tWorking with
library vendors /rKate Thornhill --tTesting and going live /
rBonnie Parks. 0aIntegrated library systems (Computer systems) 0aSystems migration. 0aLibrariesxAutomationxManage-
ment. 0aLibrariesxData processingxManagement. 7aIntegrated
library systems (Computer systems)2fast0(OCoLC)fst00975640
7aLibrariesxAutomationxManagement.2fast0(OCoLC)fst00997358
7aLibrariesxData processingxManagement.2fast0(OCoLC)
fst00997387 7aSystems migration.2fast0(OCoLC)fst01141472
7aBibliothek.2gnd 7aBibliothekssystem2gnd0(DE-588)4145276-8
7aDatenintegration2gnd0(DE-588)4197730-0 7aDatenver-
arbeitung2gnd0(DE-588)4011152-0 7aMigrationgInforma-
tik2gnd0(DE-588)4226008-5 4aIntegrated library systems
(Computer systems)0(OCoLC)fst00975640 4aLibrariesxAutoma-
tionxManagement.0(OCoLC)fst00997358 4aLibrariesxData pro-
cessingxManagement.0(OCoLC)fst00997387 4aSystems migra-
tion.0(OCoLC)fst011414721 aBanerjee, Kyle,eeditor.1 aParks,
Bonnie,eeditor.1 aRomaine, Siãon,econtributor. aBrodartb-
BRODn121371271 aBaker and TaylorbBTCPnBK0019387106 aYBP
Library ServicesbYANKn13126195 aC0bOHS

Figure 3.5: **MARC record example**

The numbers near the top of the file are an index. The first five digits indicate the length of the file and the others indicate where each character position begins and how long each field is. That means that if you don't use a specialized tool such as MarcEdit that rebuilds the index after every change, you will corrupt the file.

When librarians speak of MARC they are most often referring to the second definition, which places specific information in numeric fields that are presented in text or XML. Figure 3.6 shows a text representation of that same record.

```
=LDR  04883cam  2200661 i 4500
=001  ocn957134124
=003  OCoLC
=005  20181030121806.0
=008  170321t20172017ilua\\\\\b\\\\001\0\eng\\
=010  \\$a  2016056887
=040  \\$aDLC$beng$erda$cDLC$dYDX$dOCLCO$dOCLCQ$dOCLCF$d-
PSC$dGZN$dKSU$dNRC$dYDX$dTWT$dSDS$dWAU$dZCU$dFDA$dCHVB-
K$dOCLCO$dBDX$dNMC$dOCLCQ$dIOG$dTYC$dOCLCQ$dTXM$dCRU$dAGL
=020  \\$a9780838915035$q(paperback ;$qalkaline paper)
=020  \\$a0838915035$q(paperback ;$qalkaline paper)
=029  1\$aCHBIS$b010951010
=029  1\$aCHDSB$b006734251
=029  1\$aCHVBK$b491632606
=029  1\$aCHVBK$b494692316
=031  \\$ad
=035  \\$a(OCoLC)957134124
=042  \\$apcc
=050  00$aZ678.93.I57$bM54 2017
=070  0\$aZ678.93.I57$bM54 2017
=082  00$a025.04$223
=049  \\$aOHSM
=245  00$aMigrating library data :$ba practical manual
/$cedited by Kyle Banerjee and Bonnie Parks.
=264  \1$aChicago :$bNeal-Schuman, an imprint of the
American Library Association,$c2017.
=264  \4$c{copy}2017
=300  \\$axix, 251 pages :$billustrations ;$c26 cm
=336  \\$atext$btxt$2rdacontent
=337  \\$aunmediated$bn$2rdamedia
=338  \\$avolume$bnc$2rdacarrier
=520  \\$a"Most librarians and staff participate in at
least one data migration during their careers. And since
the new systems inevitably work differently than the
old ones and require different data to function, it's
always a challenge to plan smooth migrations that posi-
```

tion libraries to immediately leverage new system capabilities. Using step-by-step instructions and checklists, this book offers expert advice to help library
staff without programming knowledge address common con-
ceptual and technical issues encountered in migrations.
An important planning and implementation tool that will
help prevent headaches and frustration, this book offers:
a holistic view of migrating different types of library
data in ILSes, institutional repositories, DAMs, and
other types of systems used to manage data and operations; shows how to analyze, clean, and manipulate
data using skills and tools available to most libraries; demonstrates how to work with specific data types
typically encountered such as MARC, XML, and delimited
text; examines issues that affect specific areas such as
acquisitions, circulation, licensing, and institutional
repositories; addresses how to handle changes in authentication management or when moving into a wholly new
environment such as a shared catalog; thoroughly covers
testing, the final migration process, and putting the new
system into full production; offers guidance on planning
for system freeze, staff training, and how to deal with
fallout; provides step-by-step instructions as well as
useful checklists for 'go live' readiness, post-migration
functionality"--$cPublisher's website.
=504 \\$aIncludes bibliographical references and index.
=505 00$tUnderstanding the migration process /$rBon-
nie Parks --$tFormats and data cleaning /$rDavid Forero
--$tThinking beyond Excel /$rKate Hill --$tWorking with
MARC data /$rTerry Reese --$tBibliographic and item data
/$rKelley McGrath --$tAcquisitions /$rSi{circ}on Romaine
--$tPatron data and authentication /$rNathan Mealey
--$tSerials /$rElan May Rinck --$tElectronic resources
management /$rTodd Enoch --$tInstitutional repositories
and digital collections /$rKyle Banerjee --$tMigrating
to shared systems /$rAl Cornish --$tWorking with library
vendors /$rKate Thornhill --$tTesting and going live
/$rBonnie Parks.
=650 \0$aIntegrated library systems (Computer systems)
=650 \0$aSystems migration.
=650 \0$aLibraries$xAutomation$xManagement.
=650 \0$aLibraries$xData processing$xManagement.
=650 \7$aIntegrated library systems (Computer systems)$-
2fast$0(OCoLC)fst00975640
=650 \7$aLibraries$xAutomation$xManagement.$2fast$0(O-
CoLC)fst00997358
=650 \7$aLibraries$xData processing$xManagement.$-
2fast$0(OCoLC)fst00997387

```
=650    \7$aSystems migration.$2fast$0(OCoLC)fst01141472
=650    \7$aBibliothek.$2gnd
=650    \7$aBibliothekssystem$2gnd$0(DE-588)4145276-8
=650    \7$aDatenintegration$2gnd$0(DE-588)4197730-0
=650    \7$aDatenverarbeitung$2gnd$0(DE-588)4011152-0
=650    \7$aMigration$gInformatik$2gnd$0(DE-588)4226008-5
=650    \4$aIntegrated library systems (Computer sys-
tems)$0(OCoLC)fst00975640
=650    \4$aLibraries$xAutomation$xManagement.$0(OCoLC)
fst00997358
=650    \4$aLibraries$xData processing$xManagement.$0(O-
CoLC)fst00997387
=650    \4$aSystems migration.$0(OCoLC)fst01141472
=700    1\$aBanerjee, Kyle,$eeditor.
=700    1\$aParks, Bonnie,$eeditor.
=700    1\$aRomaine, Si{circ}on,$econtributor.
```

Figure 3.6: **MARC record represented as text**

For data wrangling purposes, you'll normally work with MARC as labeled text. Although MARCXML files can be manipulated much more easily than binary MARC files, converting them to text is generally much easier and is fastest—especially with very large files. MarcEdit has powerful capabilities for working with large MARC files including regular expression support, conversion, extraction, and editing, and it even supports automation. However, the command line allows you to do things even MarcEdit can't do. And sometimes it's just easier.

As is the case with MARC, when most librarians talk about formats such as Dublin Core, EAD (Encoded Archival Description), and MFHD (MARC Format for Holdings Data), they're talking about what tags contain which data—that is, it's still all plain text. This means the grep and sed commands that you've already learned are useful for extracting, analyzing, and fixing data in these formats, and you'll learn other powerful methods for working with them as text and in other container formats in other chapters.

## CHAPTER 4

Simplify
Complicated Problems

I f you're feeling overwhelmed after reading the last two chapters, don't worry. That's the most difficult material in the entire book, and you can refer back to things you can't remember. Once you familiarize yourself with the core concepts introduced in chapters 2 and 3, life will become much easier. At this point in time, you only need to know a few things:

1. **There are only two kinds of data, parseable and unparseable.** However, some structures are much easier to work with than others.
2. **Data wrangling frequently boils down to manipulating text.** That means format specific tools are often unnecessary. You can solve the vast majority of your data manipulation tasks with regular expressions and a small number of string manipulation programs.
3. **Specialized programs that are already on your computer do the real work.** You don't need to know how to program.
4. **You can combine the power of programs by using pipes and command substitution.**
5. **Complicated problems can be solved by breaking them into a series of simple steps.**

The last point is the most important. Consider the file we've been working with. It contains names that are not in consistent order, inconsistent capitalization, and inconsistent dates.

Fixing everything in a single line is possible, but that often requires advanced skills and a very ugly-looking line—just because something is possible doesn't make it a good idea. The fact of the matter is that most highly skilled individuals often break most problems into the same simple steps that a beginner would because it's easier to worry about one thing at a time, there's less chance of a mistake, and it's easier to figure out where things went wrong if the results aren't as expected.

For purposes of wrangling data, the most common ways to simplify problems are:

1. **Isolating specific data elements that need to be changed.** Breaking data into individual files that are fixed independently and later recombined, separating labeled data elements (e.g., XML or JSON) onto separate lines, fixing them, and then removing the extra lines, and other techniques can allow you to solve one problem at a time.

   It's important to keep in mind that what constitutes a specific data element depends on the specific task that you're working on. For example, if you're trying to convert all the author fields in a record set where the names were written in direct order to indirect order, you can simplify your work by directing the names to separate lines or even a separate file. However, if you're trying to figure out which records contain invalid data, it is sometimes easier to remove all the line feeds so each record is on one line.

2. **Converting data into formats that are easier to work with.** No matter what format your output needs to be in, it's often easier to work in a different format and then transform.

   There's no reason that you must work in only one format. For example, if it's easiest to work on some parts of a file as text and other parts as XML, there's no reason not to do that.

   Likewise, there's no reason to work with data in the exact form that you receive it in. For example, normalizing identifiers, punctuation, capitalization, and other methods can make solving some problems much easier.

3. **Combining simple tools and methods rather than seeking power user methods.** Improving your skills with methods you understand and regularly use will enable you to solve a wider range of data challenges than learning specialized methods that you won't use frequently enough to remember.

Isolating Specific Data Elements

By working only with what you want to change, you don't risk modifying what you don't want to change. Although the commands in this book allow you to focus on specific records and fields, it's sometimes easier to just extract records or fields you're interested in, fix them in a separate area, and recombine them.

The best method depends on the situation. Let's pretend the test file we've been working with in figures 2.1 through 2.9 was millions of lines long and we need to fix it. We could separate all the records that contain problems, but by looking at the data, we can see that all of the problems except inconsistent capitalization are peculiar to a single field.

This means that if we can isolate the name and date fields for purposes of correcting names entered in the incorrect order and dates that contain extraneous information, we can use much simpler and more reliable methods to fix them. The capitalization fix can be applied equally well on all fields, so it is already simple.

Fortunately, the cut command that you learned in chapter 2 makes it very easy to extract specific fields, which can be redirected to files that can be worked on separately. Enter the following commands as demonstrated in figure 4.1:

```
cut -f1 mytest.txt > names
cut -f2 mytest.txt > titles
cut -f3 mytest.txt > dates
grep -v "^[A-Z][a-z0-9]*, [A-Z][a-z0-9]*$" names
grep -v "^[A-Z][a-z0-9]*$" titles
grep -v "^[12][90][0-9][0-9]*$" dates
```

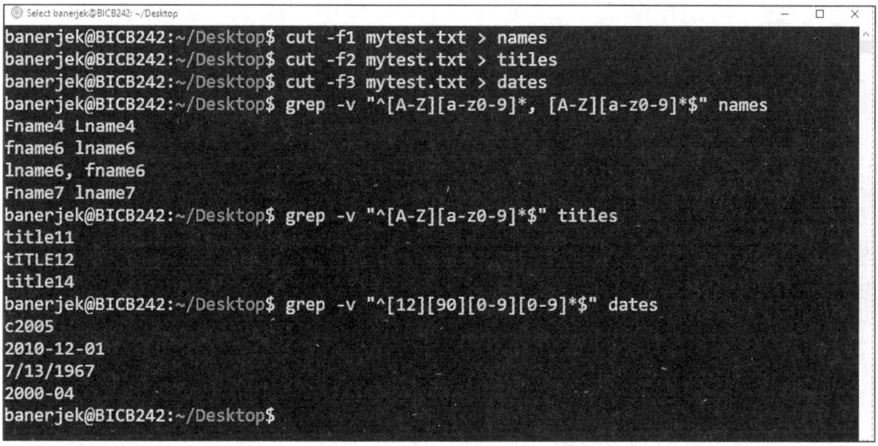

Figure 4.1: **Separating and identifying troublesome data elements**

The purpose of the `grep` commands in figure 4.1 is to identify elements that don't follow the pattern you expect. In this file, we expect that

- the name field consists of a surname that begins with capital letter, followed by a lowercase letters or numbers, followed by a comma and a space, followed a first name
- the title field consists of a capital letter followed by lowercase letters or numbers
- the date field consists of a four-year date beginning in the twentieth or twenty-first century

The `-v` switch tells `grep` only to select those lines that don't match what we're seeking. This allows you to quickly identify which variations need to be fixed. If you wanted to account for more complex name (initialisms, titles, compound names, etc.) or title (multiple words, capitalized acronyms, punctuation, etc.) structures using simple regular expression syntax, you could use multiple separate commands allowing you to look at specific aspects.

Fixing the dates will be easiest, so that's a good place to start. Our analysis reveals that all the dates contain a four-digit year, and everything else can be considered irrelevant. We can fix this in one line with

```
cat dates | sed 's/.*\([12][09][0-9][0-9]\).*/\1/'>
    dates_fixed
```

We can verify the command worked the way we intended with

```
diff dates dates_fixed
```

The `diff` command tells us about differences in lines, so it's especially well suited to the task. Any line with a less than sign indicates what was originally in the first file and a greater than sign indicates what it was changed to. To quickly view the changes in tabular format, use `grep` to select the relevant lines, sed to clean out confusing punctuation, and paste to build the table.

```
diff dates dates_fixed | grep ">" | sed 's/> //'>
    leftcol
diff dates dates_fixed | grep "<" | sed 's/< //'>
    rightcol
paste leftcol rightcol
```

Figure 4.2 demonstrates the process of fixing the dates and verifying that all our changes are good.

```
banerjek@BICB242:~/Desktop$ cat dates | sed 's/.*\([12][09][0-9][0-9]\).*/\1/' > dates_fixed
banerjek@BICB242:~/Desktop$ diff dates dates_fixed
11,14c11,14
< c2005
< 2010-12-01
< 7/13/1967
< 2000-04
---
> 2005
> 2010
> 1967
> 2000
banerjek@BICB242:~/Desktop$ diff dates dates_fixed | grep "> " | sed 's/> //' > leftcol
banerjek@BICB242:~/Desktop$ diff dates dates_fixed | grep "< " | sed 's/< //' > rightcol
banerjek@BICB242:~/Desktop$ paste leftcol rightcol
2005    c2005
2010    2010-12-01
1967    7/13/1967
2000    2000-04
banerjek@BICB242:~/Desktop$ 
```

Figure 4.2: **Fixing dates and verifying the fixes**

If you're new to regular expressions, the `sed` command is confusing. But when we break it down, it isn't so complicated.

`/.*\([12][09][0-9][0-9]\).*/\1/`	Strip out everything except a four-digit year beginning with a 1 or 2 followed by a 0 or 9.
`.*`	Any number of any characters from the beginning of the line to the next part of the expression.
`\(`	Store everything between `\(` and `\)` in `\1`.
`[12][09][0-9][0-9]`	Four digits beginning with a 1 or 2 followed by a 0 or 9. This is between `\(` and `\)`, so it is stored in `\1`.
`.*`	Everything after the four digits.
`/\1/`	Replace the entire field with the four digits captured in the search expression.
`> dates_fixed`	Send the output to the `dates_fixed` file.

As demonstrated in figure 4.3, you can fix the titles with

```
cat titles | sed 's/\w*/\L\u&/g' > titles_fixed
```

The analysis of the search and replace section of the command is

/\w*/\L\u&/g	Capitalize each word with all subsequent letters in lowercase.
\w*	Zero or more word characters (anything alphanumeric). This selects the first line.
\L	Turn the replacement to lowercase until a \U or \E is found.
\u	Turn the next character to uppercase.
&	The entire expression matched in the first field (i.e., the first word).
G	Global. If whitespace is encountered, keep searching and repeating the process on every word.

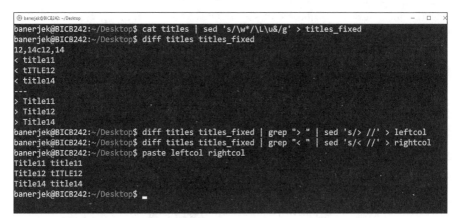

Figure 4.3: **Fixing the titles and verifying the fixes**

Fixing the authors is a bit trickier because you need to reorder and add a comma to some entries. Fortunately, sed is a great tool for this. Because we already know how to fix capitalization, we can do it all at once as shown in figure 4.4. Again, analysis of the name ordering portion of the sed command is provided:

/\(^\w*\) \(\w*\)$/\2, \1/	Convert any firstname lastname combination in direct order to surname, firstname.
\(^\w*\)	Zero or more word characters starting from the beginning of the line. Store in \1.

| `\(^\w*\)$` | Following `\1` and a space, zero, or more word characters starting from the beginning of the line. Store in `\2`. |
| `\2, \1` | Print `\2`, a comma, and `\1`. |

```
banerjek@BICB242: ~/Desktop                                          —  □  ×
banerjek@BICB242:~/Desktop$ cat names |sed 's/\(^\w*\) \(\w*\)$/\2, \1/' | sed 's/\w*/\L
u&/g' > names_fixed
banerjek@BICB242:~/Desktop$ diff names names_fixed
11,14c11,14
< Fname4 Lname4
< fname6 lname6
< lname6, fname6
< Fname7 lname7
---
> Lname4, Fname4
> Lname6, Fname6
> Lname6, Fname6
> Lname7, Fname7
banerjek@BICB242:~/Desktop$ diff names names_fixed | grep "> " | sed 's/> //' > leftcol
banerjek@BICB242:~/Desktop$ diff names names_fixed | grep "< " | sed 's/< //' > rightcol
banerjek@BICB242:~/Desktop$ paste leftcol rightcol
Lname4, Fname4   Fname4 Lname4
Lname6, Fname6   fname6 lname6
Lname6, Fname6   lname6, fname6
Lname7, Fname7   Fname7 lname7
banerjek@BICB242:~/Desktop$ _
```

Figure 4.4: **Fixing capitalization and ordering problems with names**

If more complex name variations need to be corrected, separate regular expressions could be constructed to accommodate them. For example, middle initials or names would only require a different `sed` statement so that spaces separating forenames would be handled properly. For example,

```
cat names | sed 's/^\([a-zA-Z0-9 \.\-]*\) \(.*\)/\2,
    \1/'
```

would solve that problem. Here is how that statement works:

`cat names`	Prints out names.
`| sed`	Send output to stream editor. Everything in search expression will be replaced by replacement expression, both of which are delimited by forward slashes.
`^\(`	From beginning of line, capture all alphanumeric characters, periods, and hyphens until `\)` is reached and store it in `\1`.
`\(.*\)`	Store the rest of the line in `\2`.
`\2, \1`	Print `\2` followed by a comma and a space by `\1`, effectively inverting the names.

Now that we know that all the fields were fixed correctly, we can rebuild the file with the paste command as demonstrated in figure 4.5:

```
banerjek@BICB242:~/Desktop$ paste names_fixed titles_fixed dates_fixed > testfile_fixed
banerjek@BICB242:~/Desktop$ cat testfile_fixed
Lname3,  Fname3    Title4    2001
Lname5,  Fname5    Title7    2004
Lname6,  Fname6    Title2    1999
Lname2,  Fname2    Title3    2000
Lname4,  Fname4    Title6    2003
Lname1,  Fname1    Title8    2005
Lname1,  Fname1    Title1    1998
Lname3,  Fname3    Title5    2002
Lname4,  Fname4    Title9    2009
Lname4,  Fname4    Title9    2005
Lname4,  Fname4    Title10   2005
Lname6,  Fname6    Title11   2010
Lname6,  Fname6    Title12   1967
Lname7,  Fname7    Title14   2000
banerjek@BICB242:~/Desktop$
```

Figure 4.5: **Test file is repaired**

Converting Data into Formats That Are Easier to Work With

But what if the data you're working with isn't in delimited text? What if it's in XML (eXtensible Markup Language), JSON (JavaScript Object Notation), or some other format? Most people will have difficulty working with XML tools for the simple reason that doing so requires knowledge of XQuery, a language for finding and extracting specific data elements from XML documents that works in a way that's nonintuitive for nonprogrammers. Likewise, working directly with JSON requires one to know how to manipulate programming objects—something that nonprogrammers cannot do almost by definition.

The good news is that the many techniques that work on regular delimited files also work on XML, JSON, and other formats. When you get right down to it, tags, labels, and structure are just other types of delimiters, albeit more complicated ones. This means that it's often easier to work with these files as text rather than as XML or JSON. Because most people have an intuitive grasp of plain text, it's often easier for them to use text manipulation tools even if they find some concepts (e.g., regular expressions) confusing.

There are many good reasons to treat XML or JSON as text. Both are extremely picky formats and a single invalid character in a multi-gigabyte file can cause whatever tool you're using to declare the file invalid without giving you an indication of what you need to do to fix it. On a related note, both formats (especially XML) are resource-intensive and poorly suited to processing multi-gigabyte files.

Computers are powerful, but resource utilization is a real issue. The XML specification requires the presence of a root element, which means the entire document must be loaded into memory. Moreover, XSLT (eXtensible Stylesheet Language Transformations) operations can cause a document to take up to ten times the space in memory. This means large files will tax even powerful machines. JSON is significantly less resource-intensive than XML, but serious performance issues can arise as file sizes increase. On the other hand, the plain text tools described in this book work well on files of any size.

The sed, grep, cut, and paste commands you learned earlier in this chapter are powerful and work quickly on files containing millions of records. Be aware that sed is so powerful that it is virtually a language by itself—entire books have been written about it, so you'll find help if you can't do something.

Let's take a look at an XML example. First, let's convert our original data file into a simple XML using the awk utility. awk is a very useful command that allows you to manipulate data in rows and columns.

```
cat mytest.txt | awk 'BEGIN {FS="\t";print "<records>"}
    {print "<record><author>"$1"</author><title>"$2"</
    title><date>"$3"</date></record>"}END {print "</
    records>"}' > test.xml
```

If you're interested in how the command works, here is what it does.

`cat mytest.txt	awk`	Prints out file and sends it to `awk`.
`BEGIN {`	Perform all operations between the first set of curly braces before working on the file itself.
`FS="\t";print "<records>"`	Set file separator (delimiter) to tab and print the word "`<records>`".
`{print "<record><au-thor>"$1" . . ."$3"</date></record>" }`	Print the text with `$1` representing field 1 (author), `$2` representing field 2 (title), and `$3` representing field 3 (date).
`END {print "</records>"}' > test.xml`	After last record is printed, print "`</records>` and send all output to `test.xml`.

Figure 4.6 shows the process.

```
banerjek@BICB242: ~/Desktop
banerjek@BICB242:~/Desktop$ cat mytest.txt | awk 'BEGIN {FS="\t";OFS="</td><td>";print "<reco
rds>"}{print "<record><author>"$1"</author><title>"$2"</title><date>"$3"</date></record>"}END
 {print "</records>"}' > test.xml
banerjek@BICB242:~/Desktop$ cat test.xml
<records>
<record><author>Lname3, Fname3</author><title>Title4</title><date>2001</date></record>
<record><author>Lname5, Fname5</author><title>Title7</title><date>2004</date></record>
<record><author>Lname6, Fname6</author><title>Title2</title><date>1999</date></record>
<record><author>Lname2, Fname2</author><title>Title3</title><date>2000</date></record>
<record><author>Lname4, Fname4</author><title>Title6</title><date>2003</date></record>
<record><author>Lname1, Fname1</author><title>Title8</title><date>2005</date></record>
<record><author>Lname1, Fname1</author><title>Title1</title><date>1998</date></record>
<record><author>Lname3, Fname3</author><title>Title5</title><date>2002</date></record>
<record><author>Lname4, Fname4</author><title>Title9</title><date>2009</date></record>
<record><author>Lname4, Fname4</author><title>Title9</title><date>2005</date></record>
<record><author>Fname4 Lname4</author><title>Title10</title><date>c2005</date></record>
<record><author>fname6 lname6</author><title>title11</title><date>2010-12-01</date></record>
<record><author>lname6, fname6</author><title>tITLE12</title><date>7/13/1967</date></record>
<record><author>Fname7 lname7</author><title>title14</title><date>2000-04</date></record>
</records>
banerjek@BICB242:~/Desktop$
```

Figure 4.6: **Converting a text file to XML**

If you've worked with XML before you may wonder where the XML and namespace declarations are; however, these are irrelevant for purposes here. They have been omitted to simplify the example because they don't impact the process, but you can add them.

There are many ways to analyze and manipulate XML files—you'll learn some simple but powerful methods in chapter 6. Most people use the Document Object Model you were introduced to in chapter 3, but that often requires programming skills—and at the very least, it will require you to learn a little XQuery.

Instead, we'll use a process that's similar to what we did with the tab delimited file—it's often easier to work with XML like plain text. However, there are some important differences between XML and plain delimited text.

1. A field could be missing or there could be multiple instances of a field. This means we can't just separate the data into columns and glue them back together.
2. When we perform the operations to fix the fields, we have to perform them on the entire file. This means we have to be careful not to impact fields we don't want to touch.
3. Whitespace between different tags is not significant and is usually added just for readability. This means we can isolate fields we're interested in on separate lines and remove the extra lines later.

Rather than learn new software to manipulate XML, we can use the same utilities as before. First, let's put every field on its own line using `sed` as shown in figure 4.7:

```
cat test.xml | sed 's/></>\n</g' > testlines
```

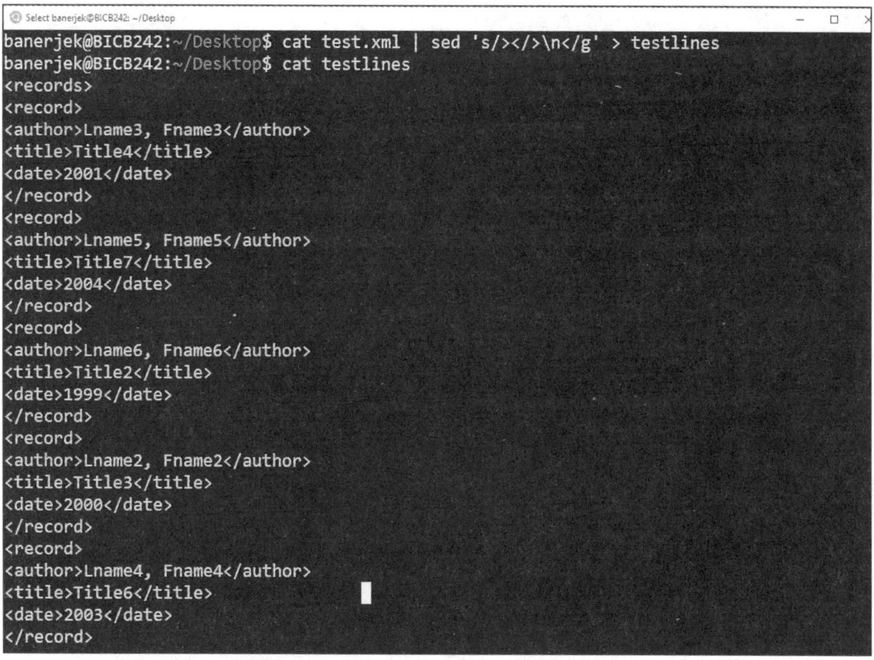

Figure 4.7: **Putting each field on a separate line**

Notice that this particular sed expression assumes tags will be next to each other (i.e., there is no whitespace between them) and that there are no tags nested that you'd want to keep together. If these assumptions weren't true, the sed command would need to be adjusted to reflect the data you actually have.

You can construct searches to find invalid entries as you did before—for example,

```
grep "<date>" testlines > dates
grep -v "<date>[12][90][0-9][0-9]<\/date>" dates
```

will find invalid dates, but because you've already seen that process, we'll go ahead and fix the file. As was the case before, we want to make sure we only modify those fields we intend to. First, let's make a copy of our file that we can work on:

```
cp testlines testlines_copy
```

Now, we can just fix the copied file in place with sed and verify we did no harm as shown in figure 4.8.

```
banerjek@BICB242:~/Desktop$ cp testlines testlines_copy
banerjek@BICB242:~/Desktop$ sed -i 's/<date>\([12][09][0-9][0-9]\).*<\/date>/<date>\1<\/date>/' testlines_copy
banerjek@BICB242:~/Desktop$ sed -i 's/<author>\(\w*\) \(\w*\)<\/author>/<author>\2, \1<\/author>/' testlines_copy
banerjek@BICB242:~/Desktop$ sed -i 's/[^ >]\+/\L\u&/g' testlines_copy
banerjek@BICB242:~/Desktop$ diff testlines testlines_copy | grep "> " | sed 's/> //' > leftcol
banerjek@BICB242:~/Desktop$ diff testlines testlines_copy | grep "< " | sed 's/< //' > rightcol
banerjek@BICB242:~/Desktop$ paste leftcol rightcol
<author>Lname4, Fname4</author>    <author>Fname4 Lname4</author>
<date>C2005</date>          <date>c2005</date>
<author>Lname6, Fname6</author>    <author>fname6 lname6</author>
<title>Title11</title>    <title>title11</title>
<date>2010</date>          <date>2010-12-01</date>
<author>Lname6, Fname6</author>    <author>lname6, fnameG</author>
<title>Title12</title>    <title>tITLE12</title>
<author>Lname7, Fname7</author>    <author>Fname7 lname7</author>
<title>Title14</title>    <title>title14</title>
<date>2000</date>          <date>2000-04</date>
banerjek@BICB242:~/Desktop$ cat testlines_copy |tr -d "\n" |sed 's/\(<record\)/\n\1/g' > testlines_done
banerjek@BICB242:~/Desktop$ cat testlines_done

<records>
<record><author>Lname3, Fname3</author><title>Title4</title><date>2001</date></record>
<record><author>Lname5, Fname5</author><title>Title7</title><date>2004</date></record>
<record><author>Lname6, Fname6</author><title>Title2</title><date>1999</date></record>
<record><author>Lname2, Fname2</author><title>Title3</title><date>2000</date></record>
<record><author>Lname4, Fname4</author><title>Title6</title><date>2003</date></record>
<record><author>Lname1, Fname1</author><title>Title8</title><date>2005</date></record>
<record><author>Lname1, Fname1</author><title>Title1</title><date>1998</date></record>
<record><author>Lname3, Fname3</author><title>Title5</title><date>2002</date></record>
<record><author>Lname4, Fname4</author><title>Title9</title><date>2009</date></record>
<record><author>Lname4, Fname4</author><title>Title9</title><date>2005</date></record>
<record><author>Lname4, Fname4</author><title>Title10</title><date>C2005</date></record>
```

Figure 4.8: **Fixing XML and verifying fixes with plain text tools**

Notice how the commands are slightly different in the following ways:

- -i tells sed to work directly on the file.
- Tags are all included as part of the search and replace expressions.
- The expression that fixes capitalization has been modified to prevent tag names from being changed. This part of the expression, [^ >], may seem nonintuitive. It makes sure that letters only get capitalized if they follow a closing bracket that can be followed by a space—this guarantees that only the contents of tags get capitalized and nothing else.

  Try running the sed command with a regular word character, \w, as before—you'll find that the tag names get capitalized. We could have let that happen and fixed the problem we caused in another step. Instead, however, we specified that the first character could be anything but a close angle bracket or space—this causes the \u to try to capitalize the open angle bracket leaving the actual tag name in all lower case, which is what we want.

Whitespace between tags isn't important, so we could call the file fixed. But we can also easily format the file like the original by removing all the line breaks and adding them back after each record.

```
cp testlines testlines_copy
sed -i 's/<date>\([12][09][0-9][0-9]\).*<\/date>/
    <date>\1<\/date>/' testlines_copy
sed -i 's/<author>\(\w*\) \(\w*\)<\/author>/<author>\2,
    \1<\/author>/' testlines_copy
sed -i 's/[^ >]\+/\L\u&/g' testlines_copy
diff testlines testlines_copy | grep "> " | sed 's/>
    //' > leftcol
diff testlines testlines_copy | grep "< " | sed 's/<
    //' > rightcol
paste leftcol rightcol
cat testlines_copy | tr -d "\n" |sed 's/\
    (<record\)/\n\1/g' > testlines_done
```

The sed commands may look intimidating, but that's because of the regular expressions. Once you become more comfortable with those, you can easily work on files of any size without having to write entire programs.

Notice the tr -d "\n" command that removes the newline characters after the paste command. Normally sed is a more versatile tool for changing characters. However, sed reads information line-by-line—that is, it stops reading when it encounters the newline character and can't see it. For that reason, we need to use the tr utility.

In many cases, it makes sense to convert the data itself to make it easier to work with. For example, if you're matching on ISBNs or system control numbers, strip out all the data that isn't part of the actual value. If you're matching words, normalize capitalization, spacing, and punctuation.

## CHAPTER 5

Delimited Text

W e've already looked at ways to simplify working with delimited text in chapter 4, but it's worth delving into some of the common challenges this format presents. Most people assume that all data is tabular but as we saw in chapter 2, this is not the case. From a technical point of view, we constantly work with delimited text. In this book, words are delimited by spaces, sentences are delimited by periods, and paragraphs are delimited by line returns.

All markup languages can be thought of as delimited. When you see

```
<book>
    <title>The Data Wrangler's Handbook</title>
    <creators>
        <editor>Banerjee, Kyle</editor>
        <editor>Parks, Bonnie</editor>
    </creators>
    <publisher>ALA Neal-Schuman</publisher>
</book>
```

the beginning and end tags delimit the fields—for example, `<title>` tag indicates the beginning of the field and the `</title>` tag indicates the end of the field.

Likewise, JSON also uses text in the form of braces, quotes, and colons to indicate which role each data element plays. Notice that within the editor fields, a comma delimits the forename from the surname.

```
{
    "book": {
        "title": "Migrating Library Data"
        "creators": {
            "editor": "Banerjee, Kyle"
            "editor": "Parks, Bonnie"
        }
        "publisher": "ALA Neal-Schuman"
    }
}
```

It's important to recognize the wide variety of forms delimiters can take because they frequently appear in what would otherwise be unstructured data. Because delimiters are plain text, you can use string parsing tools such as awk, sed, and grep with them. You can also use them to break complex problems into simpler components, as discussed in chapter 4.

Most people like to use Excel or other spreadsheet software to work with delimited files. For many applications, this works just fine. However, there are many situations where these methods don't work. Very large files can't be viewed in a graphical user interface without crashing the program. Even if the program doesn't crash, the process is so slow and frustrating that it's difficult to get anything done. Moreover, spreadsheet programs sometimes modify fields without your knowledge, which effectively corrupts important data, especially identifiers and dates.

OpenRefine is better than spreadsheet software for processing delimited text because it works with larger files and it doesn't modify fields. However, even OpenRefine cannot help you with certain types of common problems such as line breaks in your data. Nor will you be able to use it once files grow to a certain size.

The methods covered in this book can be used on files of any size. They make it much easier to identify and repair problematic data as well as extract and present data you're interested in. And they're much faster. The cut, grep, sed, paste, and awk commands you learned in chapters 2 and 4 will let you inspect, extract, and modify data with ease.

That said, you may encounter situations where Excel has the ability to do something you don't know how to do with these other tools (e.g., apply formulas). Fortunately, it is possible to work on very large files with Excel or OpenRefine if you split the file into smaller chunks. This will be a slower process, and you won't be able to do as many things, but often it will be enough so that you can work in a more comfortable environment. To split a file into smaller chunks simply use the split command as demonstrated below:

```
split --number=1/10 largefile
```

This command will create ten smaller files, each breaking after a line so you don't need to worry about breaking a record apart. The files can then be edited individually and recombined with cat. If you move all the files to a separate directory to work on them, you can recombine them with

```
cat * > combinedfile
```

Most of the time, working with delimited data means working with tabular data in which each line represents a record and each field is separated by one or more characters. This is often the easiest way to work with data, and even XML or JSON containing repeated values can often be converted to delimited data with the aid of multivalue separators as described later in this chapter.

CSV (Comma Separated Values)

In most cases, the delimiter will be a comma—an unfortunate choice, given how frequently commas occur in a wide variety of library fields. If you're wondering why people would use a common symbol as a delimiter, it's because it worked well in early days of data processing when numeric computer data was encoded on paper punch cards. As technology improved, CSV proved to be an efficient and human-readable way to transfer data between different systems. The very nature of the format is that it supports files of any size because they can be divided as necessary

The reason that we still use commas as a delimiter when there are many better choices is because it's difficult to transition away from functional things. Consider the QWERTY keyboard. People have known since the 1940s that the Dvorak layout is significantly more efficient and less likely to cause repetitive motion injuries. Moreover, all modern computers can be configured to use this layout in less than a minute. Nonetheless, almost no one uses the Dvorak layout. Anyone choosing to switch still has to use the QWERTY layout on any machine they don't control, so the only option is to know and master two layouts. The only thing worse than a bad standard that everyone uses is a good one that's not actually supported.

Commas and Quotation Marks in CSV Files

Sadly, the CSV format is not standardized beyond the idea that fields are separated by commas. Commas, newline characters, and quotation marks may appear in data, and different CSV implementations may handle them differently.

If possible, use a different delimiter to avoid confusion. Many programs support tab delimited data, but another character is better if tabs might appear in your data. If you can choose a non-typeable character, character 7 (bell) is a safe choice that will leave your data readable. If you can copy and paste a chosen delimiter, emoji that won't appear in your data are also a good choice. If the interface absolutely requires a typed character, pipes or unusual punctuation characters may be the best option. Multicharacter delimiters such as `thisIsaDelimiter` will also work, though many systems require single character delimiters.

If you must use commas as delimiters, always perform test loads because implementations may differ in terms of whether they even support commas in fields and if so, should they be escaped or quoted. Having said that, simply enclosing the field in straight double quotation marks (as opposed to smart quotes) will usually cause the comma to be read as field data rather than as a delimiter. The question then arises as to what happens if double quotes appear in the data. Again, the answer will depend on implementation, but the most widely supported answer is to use quotes to escape quotes as demonstrated in table 5.1.

If you look at the examples, you'll notice that this file follows two very simple rules:

1. If a field contains a straight double quote or a comma, the field is encased in double straight quotes.
2. Double straight quotes are escaped with another set of straight double quotes. This means that all straight double quotes in field data is represented with a pair of straight double quotes in the CSV file.

Table 5.1: **Escaping punctuation in CSV files**

Text to Translate	CSV Conversion
Comma, in field	"Comma, in a field"
Single smart quote ' in a field	Single smart quote ' in a field
Double smart quote " in a field	Double smart quote " in a field
Straight quote ' in a field	Straight quote ' in a field
Double straight quote " in a field	"Double straight quote "" in a field"
"Double straight quotes enclosing field"	"""Double straight quotes enclosing field"""
Double "straight quotes" in field	"Double ""straight quotes"" in field"
Double "quotes, including comma" in field	"Double ""quotes, including comma"" in field"
"Double quotes ""on one side and in middle	"""Double quotes """"on one side and in middle"

Multiline Fields in CSV Files

Some CSV implementations allow using quotes to enclose multiline fields but most do not. If your data contains multiline fields and you must transfer it as CSV, the easiest thing to do is replace the newline characters with a sequence of characters such as insertNewline and then convert the sequences back to newlines.

If it is not feasible to change the newlines in field data and your exports contain newlines, you have multiple options—the best one depends on your data. If you don't know if your data contains newlines, it's best to see how many records contain the wrong number of records so you don't spend time coming up with a solution to a problem that might not even exist.

The awk utility is very useful for this. Let's suppose you have a comma delimited field where every field is quoted.

```
awk -F '","' '/$/ {print;next;} {printf("%s",$0);}' myfile
```

This command is confusing even to systems people. All it does is look for a double quotation mark followed by the end of a line (expressed as a dollar sign in regular expressions) and it prints everything together except when it encounters the delimiter, which in this case is a double quote followed by a comma followed by another quote. If you can use a single character delimiter or there is a better way to detect the end of the line, you should use that. For example, if the file is tab delimited and the last field ends with a four-digit year in the nineteenth or twentieth centuries that is not enclosed in quotes, the expression would be

```
awk -F '/\t'/ '/[12][0-9][0-9][0-9]$/ {print;next;}
    {printf('%s, "$0);} ' myfile
```

If you can't use a regular expression to reliably identify the end of the line, your next best option is to print out all the lines that contain the wrong number of fields. For example, if you expect every line to contain three records in a quoted comma delimited file

```
awk -F '","' 'NF!=3' < myfile
```

would show you which ones don't have the right number of fields. Again, if the file were tab delimited, the command would look like

```
awk -F '\t' 'NF!=3' < myfile
```

If the number of records that need to be modified is small and the size of the file is too large for you to edit it with a text processor, you can delete the lines with the sed command. Note that using the sed command with the

-i switch will modify the file you're working on so use grep to store the lines you're removing so you can fix them later. Be sure to inspect that file to make sure it didn't remove any lines you didn't want removed!

```
grep "pattern_to_match" myfile > records_to_fix
```

In figure 5.1, we use grep to identify all lines that begin or end with something other than a double quotation mark.

```
grep '^[^"]\|[^"]$' myfile
```

^[^"]	Beginning of line followed by anything that is not a double quote.
|	OR
[^"]$	Anything not a double quote followed by the end of the line.

Then we use sed to match those exact same patterns and delete the lines

```
sed -i '/pattern_to_match/d' myfile
```

For additional safety, you could also create a new file rather than editing your original.

```
sed '/pattern_to_match/d' myfile > cleanedfile
```

If you're wondering why we're copying the lines to another file and deleting them rather than simply fixing them with awk, it's because sometimes the fix won't be as easy as it was here. In such cases, it's easier to move the records somewhere else where you can work on them and delete them from the original file.

Figure 5.1: **Detecting and fixing line breaks and other problems in delimited files**

Multivalued Fields in Delimited Files

Delimited files allow only one value per column, so if a field contains multiple values the only options are to create more columns (as shown in table 5.2) or to use a second delimiter known as a "repeated field delimiter" to identify the multiple values (as shown in table 5.3). In general, creating more columns is awkward because it requires an extra field for every single record for every single repeated field. For example, if one record contains twelve subject headings, every record needs twelve subject fields. If there are a large number of repeated fields for authors, notes, and so on, the table can become very awkward to work with and most of the entries will be empty.

As is the case with the field delimiter, the repeated field delimiter should not occur in the fields it delimits. Repeated field delimiters are not standard, so the most important thing is to make sure that whatever you use can be read by the program or system that will be ingesting the data.

Table 5.2: **Mulitivalued fields in delimited files using repeated columns**

Author	Title	Subject1	Subject2	Subject3
Lname1, Fname1	Title1	1st Subject	2nd Subject	3rd Subject
Lname2, Fname2	Title2	1st Subject		
Lname3, Fname3	Title3	1st Subject	2nd Subject	

Table 5.3: **Mulitivalued fields in delimited files using repeated field delimiters**

Author	Title	Subject
Lname1, Fname1	Title1	1st Subject; 2nd Subject;3rd Subject
Lname2, Fname2	Title2	1st Subject
Lname3, Fname3	Title3	1st Subject;2nd Subject

## CHAPTER 6

XML

S o far, we've looked at ways to process data in different formats using the same tools that we use for delimited text. But sometimes doing this is so awkward that specialized tools are necessary.

XML is one of the most popular formats for data, so you're certain to encounter it. XML is popular for a number of reasons:

- **XML is human-readable,** even by people who don't have experience with it. At its core, XML is simply plain labeled text with an obvious structure.
- **XML is portable across all platforms.**
- **XML is flexible and expressive.** XML can represent almost any type of data.
- **XML is simple.** XML has fewer than ten syntax rules and can be manipulated in any text editor.

XML also presents significant drawbacks, including:

- **XML syntax is verbose and redundant,** resulting in significantly higher storage and transmission costs.
- **Processing XML is resource-intensive.** In fact, it is so resource-intensive that it is often necessary to break it down into smaller chunks or convert it to another format.
- **XML syntax is super-picky,** so a single invalid character can render a huge file unparseable with no indication of where the problem is.
- **XML often references external files** outside one's control that cause performance and processing issues.
- **XML makes it difficult to express non-hierarchical relationships.**
- **XML encourages uncontrolled data.**

To complicate matters, the jargon surrounding XML is inaccessible to those who lack a significant technical background. Moreover, a large percentage of it is unimportant for the vast majority of purposes encountered in day-to-day work. For these reasons, this book introduces only core concepts in minimal detail for the sake of clarity. If you need more, consult one of the many books or websites on the topic. The W3 site at https://www.w3.org/XML/ isn't organized in a way that would be useful to people who are not familiar with the subject matter. However, see https://www.w3schools.com/xml/ for all the important details—it is well written and contains numerous examples to help you learn. Be aware that the W3Schools site is not affiliated in any way with the World Wide Web (W3) Consortium.

So What Is XML, Really?

Despite its name—eXtensible Markup Language—XML is not a language at all. Rather, it is a set of rules describing how to create other markup languages. A markup language is a system for using plain text tags to encode documents so that they can be manipulated by a computer.

You probably use markup languages almost every day. For example, HTML (HyperText Markup Language), the language used to display information in your browser, is the best-known markup language. Take a look at the code below, and then look at how a browser displays it in Figure 6.1.

```
<html>
   <head>
         <title>This appears in the title bar</title>
   </head>
   <body>
         <h1>This is some header text</h1>
         <p>The last two words of this sentence in the
         first paragraph are written in <b>bold text</
         b>.</p>
         <p>The second paragraph contains an ordered
         list where:
         <ol>
               <li>This is the first item</li>
               <li>And this is the second item</li>
         </ol>
         </p>
         <p>
         <h1>Notice that</h1>
         the tags rather than spacing and
         indentation influence the display. These tags
```

```
              do nothing by themselves--rather the browser
              has to interpret them. For example,
              <a href="http://google.com">this</a>
              is a link to Google.
              <ul>HTML is very powerful and it's used to
              <b>display everything you see in your brows-
              er.</b>
              </ul>
              </p>
       </body>
</html
```

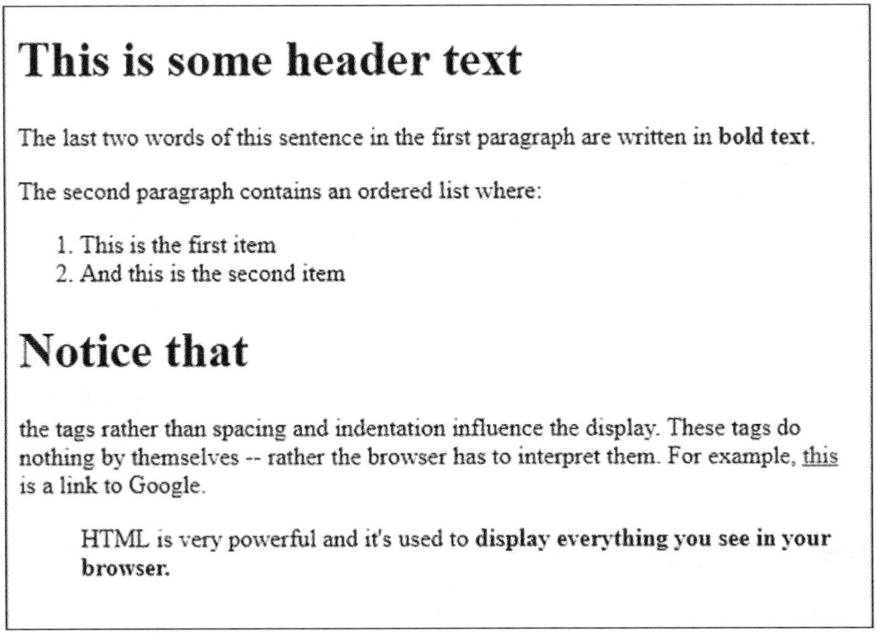

This is some header text

The last two words of this sentence in the first paragraph are written in **bold text**.

The second paragraph contains an ordered list where:

1. This is the first item
2. And this is the second item

Notice that

the tags rather than spacing and indentation influence the display. These tags do nothing by themselves -- rather the browser has to interpret them. For example, <u>this</u> is a link to Google.

HTML is very powerful and it's used to **display everything you see in your browser.**

Figure 6.1: **Using HTML to display a simple web page**

The important thing to notice is that the browser uses the tags within the text to determine what to do. The browser knows what to do with the tag because the HTML standard defines them—otherwise, the browser would have no way of knowing that the `<p>` tag indicates a new paragraph rather than purple text, the poop emoji, or something else.

Consider the XML snippet below:

```xml
<?xml version="1.0" encoding="UTF-8"?>
<MadeUpRootTag>
    <MadeThisUpToo>You can put anything you want in XML</MadeThisUpToo>
    <DidYouKnow>Even a 50 megabyte binary photo so long as it's encoded as text</DidYouKnow>
    <warning>The tags in this example mean nothing because I made them up.</warning>
    <but>But I could write a program or stylesheet to interpret them</but>
    <or>or I could follow a defined standard and use a program designed
to interpret it. For example, if I write this in HTML, browsers
could display it. </or>
</MadeUpRootTag>
```

The code above is legitimate XML even though it's completely made up—all XML does is define containers that store information. By defining standard containers for information, programmers can use the same tools to easily transfer data between very different systems and manipulate it in almost any environment. If you're reading this section, you'll probably find it difficult to perform complex operations on XML. However, you can learn to do a number of simple but powerful things very quickly and develop more skills when you need them.

What Makes XML So Useful?

Librarians often work complex structured data, so XML is very useful for transmitting information between systems and programs. For example, electronic and physical holdings, licensing, order, and repository data are often expressed in XML to support diverse purposes—even within the same system. For example, a library institutional repository might use the same XML document as the basis for a response to a mobile application, a desktop browser, an API (Application Programming Interfaces) call performing maintenance, or harvesters sending records to other systems.

Libraries find XML so useful that they started using XML before it was formally defined. In 1993, archivists developed EAD (Encoded Archival Description) to encode archival finding aids. This standard quickly experienced widespread adoption because it made it much easier for the archival community to use limited resources to work with finding aids. However, the formal XML specification wasn't released until 1996. If you're wondering how that's possible, it's because XML is a subset of SGML (Standard Generalized Markup Language), which was developed in the 1960s. XML is much simpler than SGML. EAD is a simple special-purpose language that didn't need the complexity that XML jettisoned from SGML, and it happens to conform to all the rules for creating good XML.

If you're wondering what else you can do with XML, that's a lot like wondering what you can write with a word processor or what you can do with a database. XML is a general-purpose tool, so it can be used for any purpose involving transmitting information between systems and software components.

Why Is XML So Easy?

XML is powerful and simple because it has very few rules, which gives it a great amount of flexibility. XML has a straightforward but strict syntax, namely,

1. All XML must have a root element.
2. All tags must be closed.
3. All tags must be hierarchically nested.
4. Tag names
   - are case sensitive
   - must start with a letter or underscore
   - may contain alphanumeric characters, an underscore, period, or hyphen (othing else is permitted)
   - cannot begin with the letters "xml" in any form of capitalization.
5. Attribute names must always be quoted.
6. Characters used for the XML syntax— < (less than), > (greater than), & (ampersand), ' (apostrophe), and " (quotation mark)—are not allowed in values and must be represented by <, >, & ', and ", respectively.
7. Whitespace between elements is not significant.

To use XML in its native format, you need tools to work with it. In this book, we're only going to discuss the DOM (Document Object Model) that underlies other XML standards and technologies; XPath, a language that all tools use to select data from XML documents; XSLT, a language for transforming XML documents; and XMLStarlet, a command line utility for searching and manipulating XML.

The number of tools and standards surrounding XML is overwhelming, but you'll find that you can do incredible things if you have basic familiarity with XPath, XSLT, and XMLStarlet. If you want more information about XPath, XSLT, or any XML related standards, the official World Wide Web Consortium site at https://www.w3schools.com/xml/ is an excellent resource. A wealth of information about XMLStarlet with examples can be found at http://xmlstar .sourceforge.net/docs.php.

Despite its simplicity, XML can be tricky to work with. For starters, it is extremely picky—if a single character in an entire file is invalid, none of it can be read. As mentioned earlier, the entire file must be read into memory, and common manipulations can cause the document to take up ten times the amount of space. For these reasons, it's often easier to use string parsing tools and techniques to do some of the work.

If you work with XML in library settings, you'll likely see references to "namespaces" and "schema." As is the case with many technical topics, the definitions online will help only those who already know what these things are. For purposes of wrangling data, you can usually ignore both and simply remove references to namespaces, schema, and prefixes using sed as demonstrated in chapter 2 or even a regular word processor—but there are exceptions.

In plain English, a namespace is just a way to give you context for what a term means. For example, the word "date" could refer to a specific day, a fruit, or a social engagement. In a library context, namespaces could be used to do things such as resolving name and subject conflicts when multiple authoritative vocabularies are in use.

```
<?xml version="1.0" encoding="UTF-8"?>
<root xmlns:fruit="http://fruitwebsite.com/anIdentifier"
social="http://socialwebsite.com/anotherLocation"
time=" http://timewebsite.com/YetAnotherLocation" >
    <fruit:date>Dayri</fruit:date>
    <social:date>Coffeehouse</social:date>
    <time:date>January 24</time:date>
</root>
```

In the example above, the namespaces make it clear that the context for the dates in the document is totally different. However, in practical settings where you're focused on a specific task, such distinctions either don't exist or are irrelevant. In these situations, you can ignore or remove them, depending on what you need.

Schemas describe the structure of XML documents and what is allowed in them. For example, the schema in figure 6.2 could be used to define the document in figure 6.3.

```
<?xml version="1.0"?>
<xs:schema xmlns:xs="http://www.w3.org/2001/XMLSchema">

<xs:element name="books">
  <xs:element name="book">
    <xs:complexType>
      <xs:sequence>
        <xs:element name="title" type="xs:string"/>
        <xs:element name="year" type="xs:string"/>
        <xs:element name="creators">
          <xs:complexType>
            <xs:sequence>
              <xs:element name="creator">
                <xs:simpleContent>
                  <xs:extension base="xs:string">
                    <xs:attribute name="role" type="xs:string"
/>
                  </xs:extension>
                </xs:simpleContent>
              </xs:element>
            </xs:sequence>
          </xs:complexType>
        </xs:element>
      </xs:sequence>
    </xs:complexType>
  </xs:element>
</xs:element>
</xs:schema>
```

Figure 6.2: **XML schema example**

```xml
<?xml version="1.0" encoding="UTF-8"?>
<books>
  <book>
    <creators>
      <creator role="editor">Kyle Banerjee</creator>
      <creator role="editor">Bonnie Parks</creator>
      <creator role="contributor">David Forero</creator>
      <creator role="contributor">Kate Hill</creator>
      <creator role="contributor">Terry Reese</creator>
      <creator role="contributor">Kelley McGrath</creator>
      <creator role="contributor">Sion Romaine</creator>
      <creator role="contributor">Nathan Mealey</creator>
      <creator role="contributor">Elan May Rinck</creator>
      <creator role="contributor">Todd Enoch</creator>
      <creator role="contributor">Al Cornish</creator>
      <creator role="contributor">Kate Thornhill</creator>
    </creators>
    <title>Migrating Library Data</title>
    <year>2017</year>
  </book>
  <book>
    <creators>
      <creator role="author">Kyle Banerjee</creator>
      <creator role="author">Terry Reese</creator>
    </creators>
    <title>Building Digital Libraries</title>
    <year>2019</year>
  </book>
  <book>
    <creators>
        <creator role="author">Mark Dahl</creator>
        <creator role="author">Kyle Banerjee</creator>
        <creator role="author">Michael Spalti</creator>
    </creators>
    <title>Digital Libraries: Integrating Content and
Systems</title>
    <year>2007</year>
  </book
</books>
```

Figure 6.3: **XML example**

Note that the schema shown here has been simplified greatly for purposes of clarity. Aside from the fact that the number of fields is very small, it could have also specified that only one title is allowed per book, that the year is a four-digit number beginning with a 1 or 2, that the roles attribute for creators be drawn from a predefined list, and that the creator names be in inverted order. Other rules could have been added as well.

As is the case with namespaces, schema are also generally unimportant for purposes of wrangling XML data in practical settings. The notable exception is that XSLT (eXtensible Stylesheet Language Transformations) stylesheets generally do need both schema and namespace declarations to work properly—otherwise the XSLT parser that performs the translation might not recognize the document as a stylesheet.

DOM (Document Object Model)

If you look for information on the web about XML, you'll immediately encounter references to something called the Document Object Model or DOM. If you look it up, the definitions that you'll find will be similar to the one used by Wikipedia:

> The Document Object Model (DOM) is a cross-platform and language-independent application programming interface (API) that treats an HTML, XHTML, or XML document as a tree structure wherein each node is an object representing a part of the document. (https://en.wikipedia .org/wiki/Document_Object_Model)

Unfortunately, this definition isn't very helpful. By definition, XML is in a tree structure and everything in an XML is both a node and an object. Also, the DOM is not really an API in the way most people think about APIs. It is a definition, and it doesn't do anything until a piece of software implements it.

It's easier to understand the DOM by using an example. Notice the structure of the document in figure 6.1. There is exactly one root element that serves to specify the point that searching starts from. All other elements are hierarchically nested—none can overlap. Also notice that attributes are simply something that provide more information about an element. Unlike elements that can contain other elements of any complexity as well as attributes, attributes can only contain a single value. For example, only one role attribute can exist within a creator tag and it only describes something about the creator, although we could add attributes that served different functions. However, the creators tag can contain as many creator elements as we want, and the data within the creators tag can be as complex as we want it to be. What the DOM does is give us a way to read, add, subtract, and modify anything in the document that we want.

The DOM is important because it represents the structure of XML documents, allowing you to access and manipulate individual components. Because the DOM is platform independent, the process for working with XML is very similar regardless of the tools you're using. That means that the things you learn in this chapter will help you work with XML using totally different tools in totally different environments.

The DOM is also important because it has enormous implications for people interested in manipulating large XML files. For example, because the DOM keeps everything in a tree, everything must be loaded in memory. Moreover, depending on how a tree is structured and what you want to do, adding or deleting a single value could shift almost the entire tree—something that has enormous performance implications when you're working with large files. As a practical matter, this means that whenever you need to manipulate a significant amount of XML, it's a good idea to find a way to break the problem down into steps.

Nonprogrammers can ignore most of the DOM. However, you will want to learn how to use the DOM so you can formulate XPath expressions that address different parts of XML documents. Virtually all of the XML tools you're likely to use rely on XPath, so some familiarity with it is essential if you're going to work with XML.

XPath

XPath provides a way to navigate through XML documents. For example, XPath allows you to do things with the XML shown in figure 6.1, such as listing the titles, selecting the titles where Terry Reese is listed as an author, listing titles of books written before 2018, and generally selecting parts of an XML document based on any criteria. In your regular work, you are most likely to use XPath when processing XML on the command line with XMLStarlet or when writing XSLT stylesheets (as described later in this chapter).

XPath can perform complex selections of interest mainly to those with programming skills. If you would like more information about what you can do with XPath, https://www.w3schools.com/xml/xpath_intro.asp is a good resource.

Most practical data problems can be handled with a small number of XPath expressions. XPath supports the following basic operators:

- wildcards *
- mathematical operators such as + (plus), – (minus), div (division), * (multiplication), mod (Modulus)
- equality operators such as = (equals), != (not equals), < (less than),

<= (less than or equal), > (greater than), >= (greater than or equal)

- Boolean operators (OR, AND, NOT)

XPath supports many operations, but using most of them requires programming skills. However, most practical needs can be met if you familiarize yourself with the handful of basic operations shown in figure 6.4.

/	Select root element
//creator	Select creator element regardless of where it appears in document
.	Select current node
..	Select parent of current node
//creator[role="author"]	Select creator where role = "author"
/books/book[last()]	Select the last book
/books/book[last()-1]	Select the second to last book
/books/book[year>2018]	Select books where year > 2018
/books/book/creators/creator[position()=2]	Select all creators who were listed second
//title | //year	Select title and year elements
//book/creators[creator="Terry Reese" and creator="Kate Thornhill"]/../title	Select titles where both Terry Reese and Kate Thornhill are listed as creators
//book/creators[creator="Terry Reese" or creator="Mark Dahl"]/../title	Select titles where Terry Reese or Mark Dahl are listed as creators
//creators[creator="Terry Reese"]/creator/@role	Find roles that Terry Reese played
//creators[creator="Bonnie Parks"]/creator[@role="editor"]/../../title	Identify titles where Bonnie Parks played a role as editor
//creators[creator="Bonnie Parks"]/creator[@role="editor"]/../../creators	List creators in titles where Bonnie Parks played a role as editor
count(//creators[creator="Kyle Banerjee"]/creator/../../title)	Count the number of titles where Kyle Banerjee was a creator

Figure 6.4: **XPath basic expressions**

Avoid using the // if you know the path because it searches over all nodes in the document, which drastically slows down performance. The notation has been used here mostly to make the examples easier to read.

Also, avoid relying solely on XPath to solve problems in large files because performance will be poor. Instead, break the file into smaller components. Often the easiest way to do this is convert line feeds within the data to something else, remove all line feeds between tags, convert the file to one record per line, and then process the file one line at a time. Chapter 4 describes how this can be done.

XSLT (eXtensible Stylesheet Language Transformations)

XSLT allows you to write templates in XML that extract and manipulate XML documents to create other documents. That might not sound like much, but XSLT allows you to query, perform calculations on, sort, modify, and display XML pretty much any way you like. For example, we can convert the XML document in figure 6.3 to a tab delimited file, XML input required by another system, or we can simply convert it to a web page. One advantage of XSLT is that it's just plain text, so solutions can easily be shared.

XSLT contains powerful features to which entire books have been dedicated, so you'll have to consult other resources to learn topics that go beyond the functions introduced in this chapter. Having said that, people with modest technical skills will find they can meet most practical needs by familiarizing themselves with a few basic functions. If you're interested in more detail, the W3Schools page and tutorial at https://www.w3schools.com/xml/xsl_intro .asp is well-written and easy to follow.

XSLT belongs to a family of languages known as "declarative languages." Declarative languages are special in that you describe the result rather than the procedure to follow to get to that result. SQL (Structured Query Language), which is used with relational databases, is an example of a declarative language.

The easiest way to understand XSLT is by looking at an example. Figure 6.5 contains a very simple XSLT stylesheet.

```
<?xml version="1.0"?>
<xsl:stylesheet version="1.0"
xmlns:xsl="http://www.w3.org/1999/XSL/Transform">
<xsl:template match="/">
<books>
        <xsl:for-each select="books/book">
            <title><xsl:value-of select="title"/></title>
        </xsl:for-each>
</books>
</xsl:template>
</xsl:stylesheet>
```

Figure 6.5: **XSLT stylesheet example**

If the stylesheet in figure 6.5 is applied to the XML in figure 6.3, the result is:

```
<?xml version="1.0"?>
<books>
    <title>Migrating Library Data</title>
    <title>Building Digital Libraries</title>
    <title>Digital Libraries: Integrating Content and Systems
    </title>
</books>
```

The whitespace has been added for readability—the actual string of titles is run together.

The for-each statement tells the XSLT processor to loop through all instructions until it encounters a closing tab, the select statement contains the XPath statement that points where to look, and the value-of instruction indicates that the value of title should be output. In other words, it's a loop that outputs all the titles.

But what if we wanted to list the creators and year as well? Listing the year is easy—we can call it the same way as we did the title. However, to list the creators, requires constructing another loop.

To also list the creators , we need to set up another template within the stylesheet as shown in figure 6.6.

```
<?xml version="1.0"?>
<xsl:stylesheet version="1.0"
xmlns:xsl="http://www.w3.org/1999/XSL/Transform">

<xsl:template match="/">
  <books>
    <xsl:for-each select="books/book">
      <book>
        <xsl:apply-templates select="creators"/>
        <title><xsl:value-of select="title"/></title>
        <year><xsl:value-of select="year"/></year>
      </book>
    </xsl:for-each>
  </books>
</xsl:template>

<xsl:template match="creators">
  <creators>
    <xsl:for-each select="creator">
      <creator>
        <xsl:attribute name="role">
          <xsl:value-of select="@role" />
        </xsl:attribute>
        <xsl:value-of select="."/>
      </creator>
    </xsl:for-each>
  </creators>
</xsl:template>
</xsl:stylesheet>
```

Figure 6.6: **XSLT stylesheet with nested element example**

Capturing the creators made the stylesheet more complex in the following ways.

1. Another template had to be added to the stylesheet just to handle the creators.
2. An apply-templates directive needed to be added to trigger the new template.
3. An `xsl:attribute` directive had to be entered to capture the role.

When the template is first invoked and every subsequent time an apply-templates directive is encountered, the XSLT processor invokes all the instructions on all the templates. We cannot assume that the templates are applied in any particular order—this is a feature of declarative languages such as XSLT.

The stylesheet in figure 6.6 works as follows:

1. When the stylesheet is invoked, the template `match="/"` matches the root element and instructions continue to be followed. The other template, which is looking for creators, is not matched.
2. An opening `<books>` tag is printed.
3. The for-each statement starts looping through everything in the book/book path that is a child of the root element.
4. An opening book tag is printed.
5. The `apply-templates` command is triggered by the creators element.
6. From our position in the template, the template that matches creators is invoked.
7. A loop that examines each creator is started.
8. A creator tag is opened.
9. `xsl:attribute` creates a role attribute within creator and sets the value equal to the value in the role attribute.
10. The `value-of` prints the name of the creator.
11. The creator tag is closed and the loop continues until there are no more creators
12. Title and year are printed within tags
13. The book tag is closed and the loop through the books repeats all of the above until the last book is finished

and creates the following output:

```xml
<?xml version="1.0"?>
<books>
  <book>
    <creators>
      <creator role="editor">Kyle Banerjee</creator>
      <creator role="editor">Bonnie Parks</creator>
      <creator role="contributor">David Forero</creator>
      <creator role="contributor">Kate Hill</creator>
      <creator role="contributor">Terry Reese</creator>
      <creator role="contributor">Kelley McGrath</creator>
      <creator role="contributor">Sion Romaine</creator>
      <creator role="contributor">Nathan Mealey</creator>
      <creator role="contributor">Elan May Rinck</creator>
      <creator role="contributor">Todd Enoch</creator>
      <creator role="contributor">Al Cornish</creator>
      <creator role="contributor">Kate Thornhill</creator>
    </creators>
```

```
  <title>Migrating Library Data</title>
  <year>2017</year>
</book>

<book>
  <creators>
    <creator role="author">Kyle Banerjee</creator>
    <creator role="author">Terry Reese</creator>
  </creators>
  <title>Building Digital Libraries</title>
  <year>2019</year>
</book>

<book>
  <creators>
    <creator role="author">Mark Dahl</creator>
    <creator role="author">Kyle Banerjee</creator>
    <creator role="author">Michael Spalti</creator>
  </creators>
  </creators>
  <title>Digital Libraries: Integrating Content and
      Systems</title>
  <year>2007</year>
</book>
</books>
```

Notice that when we use XSLT to convert XML documents, we need to include any tags we want output in the stylesheet. This means we can use XSLT to convert XML to delimited and other formats. For example, if we wanted to convert the XML file in figure 6.3 to a tab delimited format with authors in the first row, editors in the second row, contributors in the third row, title in the fourth row, and date in the fifth row with any repeated field separated by semicolons, the following XSLT file would work:

```
<?xml version="1.0" encoding="UTF-8"?>
<xsl:stylesheet version="1.0" xmlns:xsl="http://www.
w3.org/1999/XSL/Transform">
<xsl:template match="/">
  <xsl:for-each select="books/book">
    <xsl:apply-templates select="creators"/>
    <xsl:text>&#x9;</xsl:text>
    <xsl:value-of select="title"/>
    <xsl:text>&#x9;</xsl:text>
    <xsl:value-of select="year"/>
    <xsl:text>&#10;</xsl:text>
  </xsl:for-each>
</xsl:template>

<xsl:template match="creators">
    <xsl:for-each select="creator[@role='author']">
      <xsl:if test="position() &gt; 1">
        <xsl:text>; </xsl:text>
      </xsl:if>
      <xsl:value-of select="."/>
     </xsl:for-each>
    <xsl:text>&#x9;</xsl:text>
    <xsl:for-each select="creator[@role='editor']">
      <xsl:if test="position() &gt; 1">
        <xsl:text>; </xsl:text>
      </xsl:if>
      <xsl:value-of select="."/>
     </xsl:for-each>
    <xsl:text>&#x9;</xsl:text>
    <xsl:for-each select="creator[@role='contributor']">
      <xsl:if test="position() &gt; 1">
        <xsl:text>; </xsl:text>
      </xsl:if>
      <xsl:value-of select="."/>
     </xsl:for-each>
</xsl:template>
</xsl:stylesheet>
```

Figure 6.7: **XSLT stylesheet to convert XML containing multivalued fields to tab delimited output**

Table 6.1: **Output from stylesheet in figure 6.7 applied to XML in figure 6.3**

	Kyle Banerjee; Bonnie Parks	David Forero; Kate Hill; Terry Reese; Kelley McGrath; Sion Romaine; Nathan Mealey; Elan May Rinck; Todd Enoch; Al Cornish; Kate Thornhill	Migrating Library Data	2017
Kyle Banerjee; Terry Reese			Building Digital Libraries	2019
Mark Dahl; Kyle Banerjee; Michael Spalti			Digital Libraries: Integrating Content and Systems	2007

You'll notice many interesting things in the stylesheet in figure 6.7. Aside from containing features discussed earlier, you'll notice text is rendered within <xsl:text> tags. Because whitespace between elements in XML is considered irrelevant, tabs between fields are represented as 	 (character 9) and newlines between records are represented as &#x10; (character 10). Notice that display of semicolons between fields is controlled by test="position() > 1"—that is, a semicolon and space is placed in front of the field only when there is more than one element. As is the case with whitespace, because the greater than (>) symbol is a special character, we have to render it with the XML entity >.

XSLT can perform a wide variety of tasks including sorting, executing portions of code conditionally, converting, comparing, concatenating, trimming, reformatting, and many other functions associated with full featured programming languages. The W3Schools page at https://www.w3schools .com/xml/xsl_functions.asp describes many of these functions and provides useful examples.

Working with Large XML Files

Because working with XML is resource-intensive, you will often need to par-
tially or totally convert it to another format or at least break it into smaller
chunks. Fortunately, this is a simple matter of converting the file to one record
per line and then processing each record as a separate document rather than
parsing them together. To accomplish this,

1. **Remove the newline characters.**
   Newline characters prevent the records from being processed one per
   line, so we replace them with an unused character (in this case character 7). We will add them back in later.

   ```
   cat myfile | tr '\n' '\007' > workingfile
   ```

2. **Put a line break after each closing tag.**
   If each record ends with </record>, then

   ```
   sed -i 's/<\/record>/\n\0/g' workingfile
   ```

3. **Remove everything before the first record.**
   If each record begins with <record>, then

   ```
   sed -i 's/^.*<record>/<record>/' workingfile
   ```

4. **Remove closing root element**
   If root element is <records>, then

   ```
   sed -i '/<\/records>/d' workingfile
   ```

5. **Remove all whitespace between elements.**
   Whitespace between elements is not significant in XML, so we should
   remove it—keeping in mind that we converted all the newlines to
   character 7. The newlines and spaces within fields will not be deleted.

   ```
   sed -i 's/>[\t \x07]*<\/></g' workingfile
   ```

If you find the last command confusing, here is how it works.

```
sed -i 's/>[ \t\x07]*<\/></g' workingfile
```

sed -i 's	Work directly on the file searching for everything between the first two forward slashes.
>	Look for greater than sign (end of tag).
[\t \x07]*<	Zero or more occurrences of a tab, a space, or hexadecimal charac-ter 7 (bell) followed by a less than sign (indicating a new tag).

(continued)

/></g	Replace what was just matched with >< to restore the ends and beginnings of tags that were removed. The "g" applies the command globally (i.e., to all occurrences.

You now have a file with one record per line. Because it has no root element, you must process it one line at a time by using a simple XMLStarlet command as demonstrated in the next section. If you already have a small script named myscript that does what you want and would take a line from the file as an argument, you could process run the script on each line of the file as follows:

```
cat workingfile | while read line; do myscript $line; done
```

In this example, "line" is an arbitrary name used to store the value of each line as it is read. In the next section, you'll see a simple example using the XML-Starlet utility; in chapter 8, you'll learn how to write simple scripts. If the file is especially large, you may even want to break it down further.

6. **When done processing the file, add the newlines back.**
   Any newlines that were within (as opposed to between) fields need to be added back

```
cat workingfile| tr '\007' '\n' > donefile
```

If your file is very large, you may want to break it into pieces. The split command to however many files you like. For example, to split a large file into 1,000 smaller chunks with each file breaking on a line,

```
split --number=1/1000 largefile
```

To split a large file into smaller chunks breaking on lines so that no chunk is greater than 1 GB,

```
split --line-bytes=1GB largefile
```

If the original file contains one line per record, so will all the files created using the split command in this way. The technique of converting files so that there is one record per line is generally useful with XML because you can treat each record as a separate XML document that will consume much less memory. If you have millions of records, this may be the only viable approach.

Working with Complex XML Files

Even when files aren't particularly large, it's often faster and easier to break XML files into components. For example, consider the following patron record extracted from the local catalog

```xml
<?xml version="1.0" encoding="UTF-8" standalone="yes"?>
<user>
  <record_type desc="Public">PUBLIC</record_type><primary_
    id>banerjek@ohsu.edu
  </primary_id>
  <first_name>Kyle</first_name>
  <middle_name />
  <last_name>Banerjee</last_name>
  <full_name>Kyle Banerjee</full_name>
  <user_title desc=""/>
  <job_category desc="General Administrator">General
    Administrator</job_category>
  <job_description>Faculty</job_description>
  <gender desc=""/>
  <user_group desc="OHSU Faculty">ohsufaculty</user_group>
  <campus_code desc=""/>
  <web_site_url/>
  <cataloger_level desc="[00] Default Level">00</cataloger
    _level>
  <preferred_language desc="English">en</preferred_language>
  <expiry_date>2099-12-31Z</expiry_date>
  <purge_date>2099-12-31Z</purge_date>
  <account_type desc="External">EXTERNAL</account_type>
  <external_id>SIS</external_id>
  <password/>
  <force_password_change/>
  <status desc="Active">ACTIVE</status>
  <status_date>2015-12-31Z</status_date>
  <contact_info>
    <addresses>
      <address preferred="true" segment_type="External">
        <line1>7204 N Denver AVE</line1>
        <city>Portland</city>
        <state_province>OR</state_province>
        <postal_code>97217</postal_code>
        <country desc=""/>
        <address_note/>
        <address_types>
          <address_type desc="Work">work</address_type>
        </address_types>
      </address>
    </addresses>
    <emails>
      <email preferred="true" segment_type="External">
        <email_address>banerjek@ohsu.edu</email_address>
        <email_types>
          <email_type desc="Work">work</email_type>
```

(continued)

```
          </email_types>
        </email>
      </emails>
      <phones>
        <phone preferred="true" preferred_sms="false" segment
        _type="External">
          <phone_number>503-494-0883</phone_number>
          <phone_types>
            <phone_type desc="Office">office</phone_type>
          </phone_types>
        </phone>
      </phones>
    </contact_info>
    <linking_id>287625850001658</linking_id>
    <pref_first_name/>
    <pref_middle_name/>
    <pref_last_name/>
    <user_identifiers>
      <user_identifier segment_type="External">
        <id_type desc="Additional ID 1">OTHER_ID_1</id_type>
        <value>70712</value>
        <note>Faculty</note>
        <status>ACTIVE</status>
      </user_identifier>
      <user_identifier segment_type="Internal">
        <id_type desc="Barcode">BARCODE</id_type>
        <value>2004017833</value>
        <status>ACTIVE</status>
      </user_identifier>
    </user_identifiers>
    <user_roles>
      <user_role>
        <status desc="Active">ACTIVE</status>
        <scope desc="Oregon Health and Science University">
          01ALLIANCE_OHSU</scope>
        <role_type desc="Fulfillment Administrator">52</role
          _type>
        <parameters/>
      </user_role>
      <user_role>
        <status desc="Active">ACTIVE</status>
        <scope desc="Oregon Health and Science University">
          01ALLIANCE_OHSU</scope>
        <role_type desc="Invoice Manager">44</role_type>
        <parameters/>
      </user_role>
      <user_role>
```

```
      <status desc="Active">ACTIVE</status>
      <scope desc="Oregon Health and Science University">
          01ALLIANCE_OHSU</scope>
      <role_type desc="Invoice Operator">43</role_type>
      <parameters/>
    </user_role>
    <user_role>
      <status desc="Active">ACTIVE</status>
      <scope desc="Oregon Health and Science University">
          01ALLIANCE_OHSU</scope>
      <role_type desc="Trial Manager">217</role_type>
      <parameters/>
    </user_role>
    <user_role>
      <status desc="Active">ACTIVE</status>
      <scope desc="Oregon Health and Science University">
          01ALLIANCE_OHSU</scope>
      <role_type desc="License Manager">41</role_type>
      <parameters/>
    </user_role>
    <user_role>
      <status desc="Active">ACTIVE</status>
      <scope desc="Oregon Health and Science University">
          01ALLIANCE_OHSU</scope>
      <role_type desc="Purchasing Operator">54</role_type>
      <parameters/>
    </user_role>
    <user_role>
      <status desc="Active">ACTIVE</status>
      <scope desc="Oregon Health and Science University">
          01ALLIANCE_OHSU</scope>
      <role_type desc="Purchasing Manager">55</role_type>
      <parameters/>
    </user_role>
  <user_role>
      <status desc="Active">ACTIVE</status>
      <scope desc="Oregon Health and Science University">
          01ALLIANCE_OHSU</scope>
      <role_type desc="Vendor Manager">33</role_type>
      <parameters/>
    </user_role>
    <user_role>
      <status desc="Active">ACTIVE</status>
      <scope desc="Oregon Health and Science University">
          01ALLIANCE_OHSU</scope>
      <role_type desc="Fiscal Period Manager">45</role_type>
      <parameters/>
```

(continued)

```
    </user_role>
    <user_role>
      <status desc="Active">ACTIVE</status>
      <scope desc="Oregon Health and Science University">
         01ALLIANCE_OHSU</scope>
      <role_type desc="Work Order Operator">214</role_type>
      <parameters/>
    </user_role>
    <user_role>
      <status desc="Active">ACTIVE</status>
      <scope desc="Oregon Health and Science University">
         01ALLIANCE_OHSU</scope>
      <role_type desc="Physical Inventory Operator
         Extended">
         225</role_type>
      <parameters/>
    </user_role>
    <user_role>
      <status desc="Active">ACTIVE</status>
      <scope desc="Oregon Health and Science University">
      01ALLIANCE_OHSU</scope>
      <role_type desc="Invoice Operator Extended">48</role
      _type>
      <parameters/>
  </user_role>
    <user_role>
      <status desc="Active">ACTIVE</status>
      <scope desc="Oregon Health and Science University">
         01ALLIANCE_OHSU</scope>
      <role_type desc="Usage Data Operator">244</role_type>
      <parameters/>
    </user_role>
    <user_role>
      <status desc="Active">ACTIVE</status>
      <scope desc="Oregon Health and Science University">
         01ALLIANCE_OHSU</scope>
      <role_type desc="License Viewer">58</role_type>
      <parameters/>
    </user_role>
    <user_role>
      <status desc="Active">ACTIVE</status>
      <scope desc="Oregon Health and Science University">
         01ALLIANCE_OHSU</scope>
      <role_type desc="Selector">46</role_type>
      <parameters/>
    </user_role>
    <user_role>
```

```
    <status desc="Active">ACTIVE</status>
    <scope desc="Oregon Health and Science University">
        01ALLIANCE_OHSU</scope>
    <role_type desc="Purchasing Operator Extended">47<
        /role_type>
    <parameters/>
  </user_role>
  <user_role>
    <status desc="Active">ACTIVE</status>
    <scope desc="Oregon Health and Science University">
        01ALLIANCE_OHSU</scope>
    <role_type desc="Selector Extended">243</role_type>
    <parameters/>
  </user_role>
  <user_role>
    <status desc="Active">ACTIVE</status>
    <scope desc="Oregon Health and Science University">
        01ALLIANCE_OHSU</scope>
    <role_type desc="Fund Manager">36</role_type>
    <parameters/>
  </user_role>
  <user_role>
    <status desc="Active">ACTIVE</status>
    <scope desc="OHSU Library">OHSUMAIN</scope>
    <role_type desc="Receiving Operator">37</role_type>
    <parameters>
      <parameter>
        <type>ServiceUnit</type>
        <value desc="">RecvDept</value>
      </parameter>
      <parameter>
        <type>ServiceUnit</type>
        <value desc="">AcqDeptOHSUMAIN</value>
      </parameter>
    </parameters>
  </user_role>
  <user_role>
    <status desc="Active">ACTIVE</status>
    <scope desc="Oregon Health and Science University">
        01ALLIANCE_OHSU</scope>
    <role_type desc="Trial Participant">218</role_type>
    <parameters/>
  </user_role>
  <user_role>
    <status desc="Active">ACTIVE</status>
    <scope desc="Oregon Health and Science University">
        01ALLIANCE_OHSU</scope>
```

(continued)

```xml
      <role_type desc="Trial Operator">216</role_type>
      <parameters/>
   </user_role>
   <user_role>
      <status desc="Active">ACTIVE</status>
      <scope desc="Oregon Health and Science University">
         01ALLIANCE_OHSU</scope>
      <role_type desc="Ledger Manager">34</role_type>
      <parameters/>
   </user_role>
   <user_role>
      <status desc="Active">ACTIVE</status>
      <scope desc="Oregon Health and Science University">
         01ALLIANCE_OHSU</scope>
      <role_type desc="API Analytics Read">372</role_type>
      <parameters/>
   </user_role>
   <user_role>
      <status desc="Active">ACTIVE</status>
      <scope desc="Oregon Health and Science University">
         01ALLIANCE_OHSU</scope>
      <role_type desc="User Manager">21</role_type>
      <parameters/>
   </user_role>
   <user_role>
      <status desc="Active">ACTIVE</status>
      <scope desc="Oregon Health and Science University">
         01ALLIANCE_OHSU</scope>
      <role_type desc="Resource Sharing Partners Manager">
         239</role_type>
      <parameters/>
   </user_role>
   <user_role>
      <status desc="Active">ACTIVE</status>
      <scope desc="Oregon Health and Science University">
         01ALLIANCE_OHSU</scope>
      <role_type desc="User Administrator">50</role_type>
      <parameters/>
   </user_role>
   <user_role>
      <status desc="Active">ACTIVE</status>
      <scope desc="Oregon Health and Science University">
         01ALLIANCE_OHSU</scope>
      <role_type desc="API Fulfillment Read">223</role_type>
      <parameters/>
   </user_role>
   <user_role>
      <status desc="Active">ACTIVE</status>
```

```xml
    <scope desc="Oregon Health and Science University">
       01ALLIANCE_OHSU</scope>
    <role_type desc="Acquisitions Administrator">56</role
       _type>
    <parameters/>
  </user_role>
  <user_role>
    <status desc="Active">ACTIVE</status>
    <scope desc="Oregon Health and Science University">
       01ALLIANCE_OHSU</scope>
    <role_type desc="API User Information Read">233</role
       _type>
    <parameters/>
  </user_role>
  <user_role>
    <status desc="Active">ACTIVE</status>
    <scope desc="Oregon Health and Science University">
       01ALLIANCE_OHSU</scope>
    <role_type desc="API Resource Management Read">235<
       /role_type>
    <parameters/>
  </user_role>
  <user_role>
    <status desc="Active">ACTIVE</status>
    <scope desc="Oregon Health and Science University">
       01ALLIANCE_OHSU</scope>
    <role_type desc="Resource Sharing Partners Manager">
       239</role_type>
    <parameters/>
  </user_role>
  <user_role>
    <status desc="Active">ACTIVE</status>
    <scope desc="Resource Sharing Library">RES_SHARE
       </scope>
    <role_type desc="Circulation Desk Operator">32</role
       _type>
    <parameters>
      <parameter>
       <type>CirculationDesk</type>
       <value desc="Resource Sharing Desk">RES_DESK
       </value>
      </parameter>
    </parameters>
  </user_role>
  <user_role>
    <status desc="Active">ACTIVE</status>
    <scope desc="Oregon Health and Science University">
       01ALLIANCE_OHSU</scope>
```

(continued)

```
        <role_type desc="Electronic Inventory Operator">209
            </role_type>
        <parameters/>
    </user_role>
    <user_role>
        <status desc="Active">ACTIVE</status>
        <scope desc="Oregon Health and Science University">
            01ALLIANCE_OHSU</scope>
        <role_type desc="Physical Inventory Operator">210
            </role_type>
    <parameters/>
    </user_role>
    <user_role>
        <status desc="Active">ACTIVE</status>
        <scope desc="Oregon Health and Science University">
            01ALLIANCE_OHSU</scope>
        <role_type desc="API Label Printing Read">232</role
            _type>
        <parameters/>
    </user_role>
    <user_role>
        <status desc="Active">ACTIVE</status>
        <scope desc="Oregon Health and Science University">
            01ALLIANCE_OHSU</scope>
        <role_type desc="General System Administrator">26
            </role_type>
        <parameters/>
    </user_role>
    <user_role>
        <status desc="Active">ACTIVE</status>
        <scope desc="Oregon Health and Science University">
            01ALLIANCE_OHSU</scope>
        <role_type desc="Analytics Administrator">2200</role
            _type>
        <parameters/>
    </user_role>
    <user_role>
        <status desc="Active">ACTIVE</status>
        <scope desc="Oregon Health and Science University">
            01ALLIANCE_OHSU</scope>
        <role_type desc="API User Information Write">234</role
            _type>
        <parameters/>
    </user_role>
    <user_role>
        <status desc="Active">ACTIVE</status>
        <scope desc="Oregon Health and Science University">
```

```
      01ALLIANCE_OHSU</scope>
   <role_type desc="API Fulfillment Write">236</role_type>
   <parameters/>
</user_role>
<user_role>
   <status desc="Active">ACTIVE</status>
   <scope desc="Oregon Health and Science University">
      01ALLIANCE_OHSU</scope>
   <role_type desc="API Infra Read">238</role_type>
   <parameters/>
</user_role>
<user_role>
   <status desc="Active">ACTIVE</status>
   <scope desc="Oregon Health and Science University">
      01ALLIANCE_OHSU</scope>
   <role_type desc="Discovery - Admin">300</role_type>
   <parameters/>
</user_role>
<user_role>
   <status desc="Active">ACTIVE</status>
   <scope desc="Oregon Health and Science University">
      01ALLIANCE_OHSU</scope>
   <role_type desc="Designs Analytics">220</role_type>
   <parameters/>
</user_role>
<user_role>
   <status desc="Active">ACTIVE</status>
   <scope desc="Oregon Health and Science University">
      01ALLIANCE_OHSU</scope>
   <role_type desc="Letter Administrator">57</role_type>
   <parameters/>
</user_role>
<user_role>
   <status desc="Active">ACTIVE</status>
   <scope desc="Oregon Health and Science University">
      01ALLIANCE_OHSU</scope>
   <role_type desc="SDK Write">222</role_type>
   <parameters/>
</user_role>
<user_role>
   <status desc="Active">ACTIVE</status>
   <scope desc="Resource Sharing Library">RES_SHARE
      </scope>
   <role_type desc="Circulation Desk Operator - Limited">
      299</role_type>
   <parameters>
      <parameter>
```

(continued)

```
          <type>CirculationDesk</type>
          <value desc="Resource Sharing Desk">RES_DESK
          </value>
        </parameter>
      </parameters>
  </user_role>
  <user_role>
    <status desc="Active">ACTIVE</status>
    <scope desc="OHSU Library">OHSUMAIN</scope>
    <role_type desc="Circulation Desk Operator">32</role
      _type>
    <parameters>
      <parameter>
        <type>CirculationDesk</type>
        <value desc="OHSU Main Circulation Desk">DEFAULT
          _CIRC_DESK</value>
      </parameter>
    </parameters>
  </user_role>
  <user_role>
    <status desc="Active">ACTIVE</status>
    <scope desc="Oregon Health and Science University">
      01ALLIANCE_OHSU</scope>
    <role_type desc="Catalog Manager">206</role_type>
    <parameters/>
  </user_role>
  <user_role>
    <status desc="Active">ACTIVE</status>
    <scope desc="Oregon Health and Science University">
      01ALLIANCE_OHSU</scope>
    <role_type desc="Cataloger Extended">227</role_type>
    <parameters/>
  </user_role>
  <user_role>
    <status desc="Active">ACTIVE</status>
    <scope desc="Oregon Health and Science University">
      01ALLIANCE_OHSU</scope>
    <role_type desc="Cataloger">204</role_type>
    <parameters/>
  </user_role>
  <user_role>
    <status desc="Active">ACTIVE</status>
    <scope desc="Oregon Health and Science University">
      01ALLIANCE_OHSU</scope>
    <role_type desc="Repository Manager">29</role_type>
    <parameters/>
  </user_role>
  <user_role>
```

```
    <status desc="Active">ACTIVE</status>
    <scope desc="Oregon Health and Science University">
        01ALLIANCE_OHSU</scope>
    <role_type desc="User Manager">21</role_type>
    <parameters/>
</user_role>
<user_role>
    <status desc="Active">ACTIVE</status>
    <scope desc="Oregon Health and Science University">
        01ALLIANCE_OHSU</scope>
    <role_type desc="Catalog Administrator">205</role_
        type>
    <parameters/>
</user_role>
<user_role>
    <status desc="Active">ACTIVE</status>
    <scope desc="Oregon Health and Science University">
        01ALLIANCE_OHSU</scope>
    <role_type desc="Repository Administrator">53</role
        _type>
    <parameters/>
</user_role>
<user_role>
    <status desc="Active">ACTIVE</status>
    <scope desc="OHSU Learning Resource Center - CLSB">
        LRC</scope>
    <role_type desc="Circulation Desk Manager">221</role
        _type>
    <parameters>
      <parameter>
        <type>CirculationDesk</type>
        <value desc="Learning Resource Center">LRC</value>
      </parameter>
    </parameters>
</user_role>
<user_role>
    <status desc="Active">ACTIVE</status>
    <scope desc="Oregon Health and Science University">
        01ALLIANCE_OHSU</scope>
    <role_type desc="Fulfillment Services Manager">215
        </role_type>
    <parameters/>
</user_role>
<user_role>
    <status desc="Active">ACTIVE</status>
    <scope desc="Oregon Health and Science University">
        01ALLIANCE_OHSU</scope>
```

(continued)

```
            <role_type desc="Fulfillment Services Operator">38
               </role_type>
            <parameters/>
         </user_role>
         <user_role>
            <status desc="Active">ACTIVE</status>
            <scope desc="Resource Sharing Library">RES_SHARE
               </scope>
            <role_type desc="Requests Operator">51</role_type>
            <parameters>
               <parameter>
                 <type>CirculationDesk</type>
                 <value desc="Resource Sharing Desk">RES_DESK
                 </value>
               </parameter>
            </parameters>
         </user_role>
         <user_role>
            <status desc="Active">ACTIVE</status>
            <scope desc="Oregon Health and Science University">
               01ALLIANCE_OHSU</scope>
            <role_type desc="Patron">200</role_type>
            <parameters/>
         </user_role>
      </user_roles>
      <user_blocks/>
      <user_notes/>
      <user_statistics>
         <user_statistic segment_type="External">
            <statistic_category>Department</statistic_category>
            <statistic_note>BI.Library Main Operations</statistic
               _note>
         </user_statistic>
      </user_statistics>
      <proxy_for_users/>
   </user>
```

Figure 6.8: **XML patron record example**

In real-life situations, you're usually interested in a very specific problem—often in a single field. For example, let's suppose you wanted to make sure that the system contained institutional rather than private email addresses. Doing this with XSLT would be very difficult. However, you may remember from chapter 2 that you can use the grep command with the -v switch to identify lines that don't match a regular expression. This means you could put each record on one line as described in the previous section, and then

```
grep -v "myuniversity.edu" userfile > no_institutional
   _address
```

Lines this long are confusing to work with, so you can use `sed` or `awk` to break the file into columns that you can work with individually and rejoin them afterwards as described in chapter 4. You can use any method that makes sense to you—there's no reason to use XML tools for tasks just because your data is in XML.

In chapter 4, we used the `cut` command to break up lines. For XML, you'll normally want to use `awk` because it allows you to specify multicharacter delimiters—`cut` only allows single character delimiters. For example, suppose you wanted to just work on the email data separately for all the records. The command

```
cat userfile | awk 'BEGIN {FS="</?emails>"}{OFS="\t"}
   {print $1,$2,$3}' > usercolumnfile
```

converts the above XML into three-tab delimited columns with everything before "`<emails>`" in the first column, the XML email data in the second column, and the rest of the record in the third column. Notice that we're using a regular expression as the output field separator (denoted by the FS variable) as a delimiter. We could have used the same technique to turn all the user permissions into separate columns.

We can now work with the data in the second column using the tools of choice. When everything is the way we want, we can rejoin it again with awk:

```
cat usercolumnfile | awk 'BEGIN {FS="\t"}{print
   $1"<emails>"$2"</emails>"$3}' > finaluserfile
```

You'll notice in the output part of the command, there are no delimiters at all. We simply print the first field, the string literal `<emails>`;, the second field, which contains the email data; the string literal `</emails>`; and the third field.

What you need to do and what your data looks like determines what method works best. This is why the command line is so useful—with just a few words, you can adapt to far more possibilities than could ever be enumerated.

XmlStarlet

As you've seen in the earlier chapters, sometimes the easiest way to work with XML is to treat it like plain text. However, it's frequently the case that it's simply too awkward to be practical—for those situations, you require tools specifically designed to work with XML.

Many XML tools are available. However, we will work only with a powerful command line utility known as XMLStarlet. Broadly speaking, you can use XMLStarlet to

- manipulate XML
- search XML
- validate XML
- apply stylesheets to XML

XMLStarlet is an ideal utility for many of the tasks librarians are most likely to need, such as:

- converting XML to another format such as delimited
- extracting information from XML documents
- modifying XML documents

Unfortunately, XMLStarlet's command line syntax is nonintuitive and frankly not worth learning unless you frequently need to manipulate XML. Rather, it's easier to understand what XMLStarlet does and look up the syntax when necessary. In this chapter, we will use XMLStarlet to perform simple tasks to show how it works. In real world settings, both the XML and command line syntax will probably be much more complicated and peculiar to the task at hand. For such situations, the full documentation with examples at http://xmlstar .sourceforge.net/ can be helpful, as will be using your favorite internet search engine or online forum.

Installing XmlStarlet

Most likely, XMLStarlet is not on your machine so you'll need to install it. To install xmsltarlet on Windows or Linux, type

```
sudo apt-get install xmlstarlet
```

in a console window. If you have a Mac, use

```
brew install xmlstarlet
```

Converting XML Documents

Librarians often perform data loads, systems migrations, and analysis that requires them to convert XML to another format or manipulate its structure—tasks that XMLStarlet is well suited to assist with.

XmlStarlet is useful because it allows you to select information from, edit, and format XML documents—often in a single line. In many cases, you'll know the structure of the XML documents you'll be processing, but sometimes you won't. For example, someone needing to process the patron record in figure 6.8 probably wouldn't know the XML structure—which makes working with it much more difficult. Fortunately, XMLStarlet provides a very easy way to show the structure, as demonstrated in in figure 6.9.

```
xmlstarlet el -a finaluserfile | sort -u
```

The "el" tells the command to display the element structure, and the -a tells us to give us the attributes as well as the elements, and we're piping the output to sort -u, which sorts the output and removes duplicate lines because many fields are repeated. If we didn't care about the attributes, we could have just used

```
xmlstarlet el -u finaluserfile
```

and it would have listed the elements without the attributes, sorted uniquely for us thanks to the -u switch. As you can see, the structure is complex—this particular patron record contains 586 elements, so you definitely want to work with this the easiest way possible!

```
user
user/account_type
user/account_type/@desc
user/campus_code
user/campus_code/@desc
user/cataloger_level
user/cataloger_level/@desc
user/contact_info
user/contact_info/addresses
user/contact_info/addresses/address
user/contact_info/addresses/address/address_note
user/contact_info/addresses/address/address_types
user/contact_info/addresses/address/address_types/address_
    type
user/contact_info/addresses/address/address_types/address_
    type/@desc
```

(continued)

```
  user/contact_info/addresses/address/city
user/contact_info/addresses/address/country
user/contact_info/addresses/address/country/@desc
user/contact_info/addresses/address/line1
user/contact_info/addresses/address/postal_code
user/contact_info/addresses/address/@preferred
user/contact_info/addresses/address/@segment_type
user/contact_info/addresses/address/state_province
user/contact_info/emails
user/contact_info/emails/email
user/contact_info/emails/email/email_address
user/contact_info/emails/email/email_types
user/contact_info/emails/email/email_types/email_type
user/contact_info/emails/email/email_types/email_type/@desc
user/contact_info/emails/email/@preferred
user/contact_info/emails/email/@segment_type
user/contact_info/phones
user/contact_info/phones/phone
user/contact_info/phones/phone/phone_number
user/contact_info/phones/phone/phone_types
user/contact_info/phones/phone/phone_types/phone_type
user/contact_info/phones/phone/phone_types/phone_type/@desc
user/contact_info/phones/phone/@preferred
user/contact_info/phones/phone/@preferred_sms
user/contact_info/phones/phone/@segment_type
user/expiry_date
user/external_id
  user/first_name
user/force_password_change
user/full_name
user/gender
user/gender/@desc
user/job_category
user/job_category/@desc
user/job_description
user/last_name
user/linking_id
user/middle_name
user/password
user/preferred_language
user/preferred_language/@desc
user/pref_first_name
user/pref_last_name
user/pref_middle_name
user/primary_id
user/proxy_for_users
user/purge_date
user/record_type
```

```
user/record_type/@desc
user/status
user/status_date
user/status/@desc
user/user_blocks
user/user_group
user/user_group/@desc
user/user_identifiers
user/user_identifiers/user_identifier
user/user_identifiers/user_identifier/id_type
user/user_identifiers/user_identifier/id_type/@desc
user/user_identifiers/user_identifier/note
user/user_identifiers/user_identifier/@segment_type
user/user_identifiers/user_identifier/status
user/user_identifiers/user_identifier/value
user/user_notes
user/user_roles
user/user_roles/user_role
user/user_roles/user_role/parameters
user/user_roles/user_role/parameters/parameter
user/user_roles/user_role/parameters/parameter/type
user/user_roles/user_role/parameters/parameter/value
user/user_roles/user_role/parameters/parameter/value/@desc
user/user_roles/user_role/role_type
user/user_roles/user_role/role_type/@desc
user/user_roles/user_role/scope
user/user_roles/user_role/scope/@desc
user/user_roles/user_role/status
user/user_roles/user_role/status/@desc
user/user_statistics
user/user_statistics/user_statistic
user/user_statistics/user_statistic/@segment_type
user/user_statistics/user_statistic/statistic_category
user/user_statistics/user_statistic/statistic_note
user/user_title
user/user_title/@desc
user/web_site_url
```

Figure 6.9: **Analyzing the structure of XML with XMLStarlet**

To extract data from the XML file, all you need to do is tell XMLStarlet the appropriate XPath expressions. For example, if you wanted to extract the last name, first name, a tab, and then the preferred email address, the command

```
xmlstarlet sel -t -m '/user' -v 'last_name' -o ', ' -v
    'first_name' -o "$(echo -e '\t')" -v 'contact_info/
    emails/email[@preferred="true"]/email_address' -n
    finaluserfile
```

would work. To understand how the command works, `sel` tells `xmlstarlet` that we're selecting data (as opposed to editing, transforming, analyzing, or validating it). The `-t` indicates that we're applying a template. The template looks to `-m` to know which XPath expression to match and from there uses the `-v` to understand which values to select. The `-m` can be eliminated, but then the full path needs to be included for every element, which can result in longer and more complex commands. The `-o` indicates that a string literal will be output—we output a comma followed by a space between the name elements and a tab character after the first name.

Notice that we used command substitution as described in chapter 2 to print the tab because we weren't able to type it on the command line. This same technique could be used to modify any value using another command or a script. This means you have the ability to use any tool you like on any individual element or value.

Also notice that the XPath statement for the email only selects the email address if the preferred attribute is set to true. The `-n` at the end just prints a blank line after the output.

It's generally easiest to use XMLStarlet with command parameters when it's not necessary to select or modify much in the original XML. This example is relatively simple, but the commands can get confusing as the XML and your requirements become more complex, particularly if you need to do conditional selection or manipulation when some elements are empty, repeated, or contain child elements.

In such cases, it's often easier to use XMLStarlet to apply stylesheets than it is to use the command syntax. For example, the following stylesheet:

```
<?xml version="1.0" encoding="UTF-8"?>
<xsl:stylesheet version="1.0" xmlns:xsl="http://
    www.w3.org/1999/XSL/Transform">
<xsl:template match="/user">
<xsl:value-of select="last_name"/>
<xsl:text>, </xsl:text>
<xsl:value-of select="first_name"/>
```

```
<xsl:text>&#x9;</xsl:text>
<xsl:value-of select="contact_info/emails/email
  [@preferred='true']/email_address"/>
</xsl:template>
</xsl:stylesheet>
```

could be applied with the command

```
xmlstarlet tr mystylesheet.xsl -n finaluserfile
```

to achieve the same result with the XML file in figure 6.9. Notice the "tr" option indicating a transformation using an XSLT stylesheet. Also notice that the tab has been entered as hexadecimal entity 	 (character 9) within the <xsl:text> element. You can also insert, update, rename, move, and delete XML elements from the command line, but it's usually easier to accomplish all but minor changes via XSLT.

You can perform minor changes as follows.

Add an element:

```
cat xmldoc | xmlstarlet ed -s '/path_to_ele-
  ment[not(new_element)]' -t elem -n new_attribute -v
  'New value'
```

Add an attribute:

```
cat xmldoc | xmlstarlet ed -s '/path_to_element' -t
  attr -n new_attribute -v 'New value'
```

Delete an element, attribute, or anything based on XPath expressions.

```
cat xmldoc | xmlstarlet ed -d '/XPath_Expression'
```

Don't worry about memorizing XMLStarlet's syntax. You only need to know that it allows you to analyze, select, and modify data from the command line or by applying stylesheets.

When working with large files containing many XML records, the easiest and most efficient approach is usually to break them into one record per line as described earlier in this chapter and send each to XMLStarlet using the scripting techniques discussed in chapter 8.

## CHAPTER 7

JSON
(JavaScript Object Notation)

J SON is a simple method of structuring data so that it can easily be manipulated by computers. At its core, JSON is labeled text data. However, unlike regular labeled data, which only provides for a name and a value in two columns, JSON can express hierarchical and multivalued data elements. As such, JSON provides much more sophisticated access than textual strings. At the same time, it's easier to work with than XML and requires fewer resources.

JSON is often presented as a superior alternative to XML. However, it is awkward with nonhierarchical data, inappropriate for data best expressed using a markup language, and requires programming skills if the structure isn't simple. However, it's worth knowing because it's a very useful format and it's often the only format you can get data in.

The rules for constructing JSON are simple:

1. **Data is expressed in key/value pairs** consisting of a field name in double quotes, followed by a colon, followed by a value.

    At its core, a key/value pair is just two values. The one designated as the "key" points to the value. For example, in the key/value pair

    ```
    "Title" : "Migrating Library Data"
    ```

    "Title" is the key that points to "Migrating Library Data." Programming languages use keys to access values.

2. **Values can be strings, objects, arrays, or literals.**

    This means values may be very simple or complex. A string is typically numbers, letters, and punctuation but can contain other characters. Arrays are collections of the same type of variable that can be accessed through an index. In this book, you'll normally see notation like `myvariable[2]` to access the third item within the `myvariable` array (the first item is in `myvariable[0]`). For purposes of this book, an object is any combination of variables, arrays, and other objects. A literal is a value.

3. **Objects begin and end with curly braces ({}).**

   For JSON purposes, "object" is an all-encompassing term used to refer to any combination of strings, arrays, literals, and other objects that can be accessed with an identifier.

4. **Arrays begin and end with square brackets ([]).**

   In JSON, an array is a data structure that is a collection of strings, numbers, Booleans, objects, or other arrays.

5. **Strings must be in double quotes.**

6. **Data is separated by commas.**

That sounds abstract and confusing, so let's look at an example.

```
{
  "StringKey": "Anything you can type",
  "AnotherStringKey": "More string data",
  "ArrayKeyContainingStrings": [
    "item1",
    "item2",
    "item3"
  ],
  "ObjectKeyContainingPerson": {
    "StringKeyContainingName": "Kyle",
    "IntegerKeyContainingAge": 51,
    "ObjectKeyContainingPets": {
      "ArrayKeyContainingDogs": [
        "Powder",
        "Keiko"
      ],
      "ArrayKeyContainingCats": [
        "Peet",
        "Jethro",
        "Triscuit"
      ]
    }
  }
}
```

Figure 7.1: **Simple JSON Example**

Figure 7.1 contains strings, integers, arrays, and objects. Everything containing the word "key" is in fact a key used to access various strings, objects, arrays, and integers. All of the names of keys are arbitrary—although their names here include what they do, that is only for illustrative purposes. The indentation is for readability and is not required. As is the case with XML, whitespace between elements is not significant.

At the most basic level, you use keys to access values. With JSON, the structure is much more complex than with delimited files, so accessing elements that we want is also more complicated. As is the case with XML, removing line breaks and using regular expressions is sometimes a viable approach. However, except with all but the simplest JSON, it's normally easier to use a specialized tool.

JSON is designed for programmers, but the `jq` command line utility will allow you to do amazing things in a single line. `jq` is an incredibly powerful utility that is virtually a programming language by itself. Once you familiarize yourself with the information about `jq` presented here, you can find a full manual at https://stedolan.github.io/jq/manual/. Be aware that nonprogrammers may have difficulty reading it.

If the JSON within figure 7.1 is stored within the file "yfile.json, the command

```
cat myfile.json | jq '.StringKey, .AnotherStringKey'
```

would result in the output:

```
"Anything you can type"
"More string data"
```

Notice the following about the command:

- A dot precedes both keys. If we would have just output a dot, the entire JSON document would have printed.
- There is a comma between the two elements. When you want to output multiple elements and strings, they must be separated with commas.
- The values of `StringKey` and `AnotherStringKey` appear on separate lines and are enclosed in quotes.

If you had tried to print out the ArrayKeyContainingStrings with

```
cat myfile.json | jq '.StringKey, .AnotherStringKey,
    .ArrayKeyContainingStrings'
```

you'd get

```
"Anything you can type"
"More string data"
[
"item1",
"item2",
"item3"
]
```

The reason the values are appearing in quotes and brackets is that jq is designed to output JSON—all it lacks here are labels, which we could have added. For most library work, you're probably more interested in converting JSON to something else—maybe plain text—than turning it into other JSON. If we didn't want the brackets for the items, the command

```
cat myfile.json | jq '.StringKey, .AnotherStringKey,
    .ArrayKeyContainingStrings[]'
```

would result in

```
"Anything you can type"
"More string data"
"item1"
"item2"
"item3"
```

Notice that the brackets and commas have disappeared. This is because the [] following ArrayKeyCountingStrings tells jq to print all the elements. If we want all the output on one line in a tab delimited format, the command

```
cat myfile.json | jq -r '[.StringKey, .AnotherStringKey,
    .ArrayKeyContainingStrings[]] | @tsv'
```

creates the output

```
Anything you can type More string data item1 item2
    item3
```

Notice the following in the above command:

- The -r switch tells jq to output raw data rather than in JSON format. This gets rid of the quotes.
- The left bracket is in front of StringKey and the right bracket after ArrayKeyContainingStrings[] encloses the entire output in brackets, converting it to an array that can be sent to the @tsv option, which converts it to tab delimited.

- Pipes are used within `jq` the same way they are used in the command line—that is, the output from whatever is in front of the pipe is input for whatever follows the pipe. In this case, an array is converted to tab delimited.

But what if `ArrayKeyContainingStrings` is a repeated field that you want to output as a single field containing a semicolon as a repeated field delimiter? Fortunately, `jq` makes that easy.

```
cat myfile.json | jq -r '[.StringKey, .AnotherStringKey,
    (.ArrayKeyContainingStrings | join(";"))] | @tsv'
```

Which generates the following output:

```
Anything you can type More string data item1;item2;item3
```

Notice the following about the command above.

- `ArrayKeyContainingStrings` is now piped to the `join` command, which specifies a semicolon as a delimiter separating the elements that were joined.
- `ArrayKeyContainingStrings` and `join` are both surrounded by parenthesis separating them from the rest of the expression. This means only the `ArrayKeyContainingStrings` will be subject to the `join` command.
- The brackets following `ArrayKeyContainingStrings` has been removed. This is because `join` only works on arrays and the brackets cause the individual members (i.e., strings) to be printed with `join` doesn't know how to work with.

jq has powerful selection capabilities. Let's suppose we wanted to get a list of the cats that Kyle has. The following command would produce such a list.

```
cat myfile.json | jq '.ObjectKeyContainingPerson |
    select(.StringKeyContainingName | test("Kyle")) |
    .ObjectKeyContainingPets.ArrayKeyContainingCats'
[
"Peet",
"Jethro",
"Triscuit"
]
```

As you can see, using `jq` is tricky even with simple data and it gets more complicated quickly. But you can also see it does an amazing amount of work in one line. Let's try a more complicated real-world example. Consider figure 7.2, which was output from a digital repository.

```
{
  "id": 11801,
  "url": "https://digitalcollections.ohsu.edu/api/
items/11801",
  "public": true,
  "featured": false,
  "added": "2014-02-27T22:21:16+00:00",
  "modified": "2014-04-17T22:39:40+00:00",
  "item_type": {
    "id": 6,
    "url": "https://digitalcollections.ohsu.edu/api/item
        _types/6",
    "name": "Still Image",
    "resource": "item_types"
  },
  "collection": {
    "id": 2,
    "url": "https://digitalcollections.ohsu.edu/api/
        collections/2",
    "resource": "collections"
  },
  "owner": {
    "id": 1,
    "url": "https://digitalcollections.ohsu.edu/api/
users/1",
    "resource": "users"
  },
  "files": {
    "count": 1,
    "url": "https://digitalcollections.ohsu.edu/api/
        files?item=11801",
    "resource": "files"
  },
  "tags": [
    {
      "id": 12435,
      "url": "https://digitalcollections.ohsu.edu/api/
        tags/12435",
      "name": "Lovejoy, Esther Clayson Pohl, M.D., 1869-
        1967",
      "resource": "tags"
    },
    {
      "id": 1560,
      "url": "https://digitalcollections.ohsu.edu/api/
        tags/1560",
      "name": "Physicians, Women",
      "resource": "tags"
    },
```

```
  {
    "id": 1421,
    "url": "https://digitalcollections.ohsu.edu/api/
       tags/1421",
    "name": "Portraits",
    "resource": "tags"
  }
],
"element_texts": [
  {
    "html": false,
    "text": "Esther Pohl Lovejoy, M.D.",
    "element_set": {
      "id": 1,
      "url": "https://digitalcollections.ohsu.edu/api/
         element_sets/1",
      "name": "Dublin Core",
      "resource": "element_sets"
    },
    "element": {
      "id": 50,
      "url": "https://digitalcollections.ohsu.edu/api/
         elements/50",
      "name": "Title",
      "resource": "elements"
    }
  },
  {
    "html": false,
    "text": "1894",
    "element_set": {
      "id": 1,
      "url": "https://digitalcollections.ohsu.edu/api/
         element_sets/1",
      "name": "Dublin Core",
      "resource": "element_sets"
    },
    "element": {
      "id": 40,
      "url": "https://digitalcollections.ohsu.edu/api/
         elements/40",
      "name": "Date",
      "resource": "elements"
    }
  },
  {
    "html": false,
    "text": "Historical Image Collection",
```

```
      "element_set": {
        "id": 1,
        "url": "https://digitalcollections.ohsu.edu/api/
            element_sets/1",
        "name": "Dublin Core",
        "resource": "element_sets"
      },
      "element": {
        "id": 48,
        "url": "https://digitalcollections.ohsu.edu/api/
            elements/48",
        "name": "Source",
        "resource": "elements"
      }
    },
    {
      "html": false,
      "text": "portraits",
      "element_set": {
        "id": 1,
        "url": "https://digitalcollections.ohsu.edu/api/
            element_sets/1",
        "name": "Dublin Core",
        "resource": "element_sets"
      },
      "element": {
        "id": 79,
        "url": "https://digitalcollections.ohsu.edu/api/
            elements/79",
        "name": "Medium",
        "resource": "elements"
      }
    },
    {
      "html": false,
      "text": "photographs",
      "element_set": {
        "id": 1,
        "url": "https://digitalcollections.ohsu.edu/api/
            element_sets/1",
        "name": "Dublin Core",
        "resource": "element_sets"
      },
      "element": {
        "id": 79,
        "url": "https://digitalcollections.ohsu.edu/api/
            elements/79",
        "name": "Medium",
```

```
          "resource": "elements"
        }
      },
      {
        "html": false,
        "text": "Lovejoy, Esther Clayson Pohl, M.D., 1869-
1967\
          r\n",
        "element_set": {
          "id": 1,
          "url": "https://digitalcollections.ohsu.edu/api/
              element_sets/1",
          "name": "Dublin Core",
          "resource": "element_sets"
        },
        "element": {
          "id": 49,
          "url": "https://digitalcollections.ohsu.edu/api/
              elements/49",
          "name": "Subject",
          "resource": "elements"
        }
      },
      {
        "html": false,
        "text": "Physicians, Women",
        "element_set": {
          "id": 1,
          "url": "https://digitalcollections.ohsu.edu/api/
              element_sets/1",
          "name": "Dublin Core",
          "resource": "element_sets"
        },
        "element": {
          "id": 49,
          "url": "https://digitalcollections.ohsu.edu/api/
              elements/49",
          "name": "Subject",
          "resource": "elements"
        }
      },
      {
        "html": false,
        "text": "Portraits",
        "element_set": {
          "id": 1,
          "url": "https://digitalcollections.ohsu.edu/api/
              element_sets/1",
```

```
        "name": "Dublin Core",
        "resource": "element_sets"
    },
    "element": {
      "id": 49,
      "url": "https://digitalcollections.ohsu.edu/api/
          elements/49",
      "name": "Subject",
      "resource": "elements"
    }
  },
  {
    "html": false,
    "text": "Digital scan of photograph of Esther Clayson
        Pohl Lovejoy, M.D.",
    "element_set": {
      "id": 1,
      "url": "https://digitalcollections.ohsu.edu/api/
          element_sets/1",
      "name": "Dublin Core",
      "resource": "element_sets"
    },
    "element": {
      "id": 41,
      "url": "https://digitalcollections.ohsu.edu/api/
          elements/41",
      "name": "Description",
      "resource": "elements"
    }
  },
  {
    "html": false,
    "text": "lovejoy_esther_pohl_md_2.jpg",
    "element_set": {
      "id": 1,
      "url": "https://digitalcollections.ohsu.edu/api/
          element_sets/1",
      "name": "Dublin Core",
      "resource": "element_sets"
    },
    "element": {
      "id": 43,
      "url": "https://digitalcollections.ohsu.edu/api/
          elements/43",
      "name": "Identifier",
      "resource": "elements"
    }
  },
```

```json
{
  "html": false,
  "text": "Still Image",
  "element_set": {
    "id": 1,
    "url": "https://digitalcollections.ohsu.edu/api/
        element_sets/1",
    "name": "Dublin Core",
    "resource": "element_sets"
  },
  "element": {
    "id": 51,
    "url": "https://digitalcollections.ohsu.edu/api/
        elements/51",
    "name": "Type",
    "resource": "elements"
  }
},
{
  "html": false,
  "text": "doi:10.6083/M4NV9GN2",
  "element_set": {
    "id": 1,
    "url": "https://digitalcollections.ohsu.edu/api/
        element_sets/1",
    "name": "Dublin Core",
    "resource": "element_sets"
  },
  "element": {
    "id": 43,
    "url": "https://digitalcollections.ohsu.edu/api/
        elements/43",
    "name": "Identifier",
    "resource": "elements"
  }
},
{
  "html": false,
  "text": "COPYRIGHT NOT EVALUATED http://rightsstate-
ments
      .org/vocab/CNE/1.0/",
  "element_set": {
    "id": 1,
    "url": "https://digitalcollections.ohsu.edu/api/
        element_sets/1",
    "name": "Dublin Core",
    "resource": "element_sets"
  },
```

```
          "element": {
            "id": 47,
            "url": "https://digitalcollections.ohsu.edu/api/
                elements/47",
            "name": "Rights",
            "resource": "elements"
          }
        },
        {
          "html": false,
          "text": "You may use these materials on a fair use
            basis, in accordance with Title 17, Section 107 of
            U.S. copyright law. For other uses, please contact
            OHSU Historical Collections & Archives for permis-
            sion to reproduce, publish, or otherwise distrib-
            ute images or other materials from this collection.
            We request that any reproduction of these images
            include an attribution to OHSU Historical Collec-
            tions & Archives as the source of this material.",
          "element_set": {
            "id": 1,
            "url": "https://digitalcollections.ohsu.edu/api/ele-
ment_sets/1",
            "name": "Dublin Core",
            "resource": "element_sets"
          },
          "element": {
            "id": 47,
            "url": "https://digitalcollections.ohsu.edu/api/ele-
ments/47",
            "name": "Rights",
            "resource": "elements"
          }
        }
      ],
    "extended_resources": {
      "exhibit_pages": {
        "count": 0,
        "url": "https://digitalcollections.ohsu.edu/api/
exhibit_pages?item=11801",
        "resource": "exhibit_pages"
      }
    }
}
```

Figure 7.2: **More complex JSON example**

Let's suppose you need to convert the output to tab delimited display with title in the first column, date in the second, and the subjects separated by semi-colons in the third.

```
cat myfile.json | jq -r '.element_texts | [(.[] |
   (select(.element.name=="Title"), (select(.element.
   name=="Date"))) | .text), (map(select(.element.
   name=="Subject") | .text) | join(";"))] | @tsv'
```

generates the necessary output, namely,

Esther Pohl Lovejoy, M.D	1894	Lovejoy, Esther Clayson Pohl, M.D., 1869–1967; Physicians, Women;Portraits

The command line looks intimidating, but if you look more closely, you'll see it's surprisingly simple. In broad terms,

- .[] iterates through all items in element_texts that and prints text value for items we're interested in that have only one element (title and date).
- The map statement converts the strings from the repeatable field subjects to an array so they can be concatenated with semicolons using the join command effectively making them a single string like the title and date.
- The entire line of output is enclosed in brackets to convert it to an array so it can be sent to the @tsv statement, which converts it to tab delimited format.

If we look at the command split over multiple lines so it's easier to read, we get:

```
.element_texts
| [(.[]
| ((select(.element.name=="Title"),
(select(.element.name=="Date")))
| .text)),
(map(select(.element.name=="Subject") | .text)
| join(";") ) ]
| @tsv
```

A lengthier and less elegant but easier to understand method that achieves the same result would be

```
cat myfile.json | jq '[(.element_texts[] | (select
    (.element.name=="Title") | .text)), (.element_
    texts[] |(select(.element.name=="Date") | .text)),
    ([.element_texts[] | (select(.element.name==
    "Subject") | .text)] | join(";"))]| @tsv'
```

Rather than having elements with commonalities share a process and mapping repeated elements, we simply give every column its own process and explicitly call the individual elements and surround the repeated subject elements in brackets.

Again, now broken over multiple lines to make it more understandable,

```
[
(.element_texts[]
| (select(.element.name=="Title")
| .text)),
(.element_texts[]
| (select(.element.name=="Date")
| .text)),
([
.element_texts[]
| (select(.element.name=="Subject")
| .text)
]
| join(";"))
]
| @tsv'
```

The important thing to notice with both solutions is they use parentheses to group processes and use pipes to filter data to, within, and out of processes. As you can see, a little bit of knowledge really goes a long way toward making short work of complicated-looking problems.

So far, all of our examples have printed values associated with keys. But what if you needed to print the keys themselves? With our example above, you'd type

```
cat myfile.json | jq -r 'keys[] as $k | "\($k)"'
```

and you'll get the output

```
added
collection
element_texts
extended_resources
featured
files
id
item_type
modified
owner
public
tags
url
```

If you want to see the actual values as well as the keys, the command becomes

```
cat myfile.json | jq -r 'keys[] as $k | "\($k), \(.[$k])"'
```

If you try that command, you'll notice the output is very easy to parse using commands you already know, such as sed and grep.

If you're not accustomed to jq, the punctuation can be intimidating and might require trial and error. However, the important thing to remember is that if it's necessary to do something with JSON, jq can probably do what you need. If you're really feeling lost and want help with jq, online forums can be very useful. The https://stackoverflow.com site is a particularly good resource.

## CHAPTER 8

Scripting

One of the most useful aspects of the command line is the ability to write scripts. As we saw in chapter 2, a script is just a plain text file containing instructions. These instructions can be commands, programs, program code, or other scripts. Scripts allow you to combine the power of different programs on your machine that accept input from arguments, pipes, and files.

In chapter 1, you listed the files on your desktop using the command line. To write a script, change into your desktop directory. From here, you can edit, create, and modify files using the same GUI editor you've always used. If you do use a GUI, be aware that all single and double quotes must be straight quotes—if you use "smart quotes," you'll get errors when you try to run your scripts. You can also use a command line editor—nano is a good choice for people who are new to scripting. Just type

```
nano myfile
```

to create or edit `myfile`. Nano contains menus, so you don't need instructions to use it. The only thing that's not completely obvious to new users is that in the menus, the "^" is used to refer to the control key and "M-" refers to the meta key—typically, the option, escape, or alt key depending on the computer you're using. If you're new to scripting, you may want to avoid the vi editor despite the fact that it's a favorite among programmers and systems people. The text editor vi is very powerful and fast, but it's unfriendly and takes a long time to master.

Regardless of which method you choose, enter the following in the file, save, and exit.

```
curl 'https://viaf.org/viaf/34791410/viaf.xml' > viaf.xml
```

The `curl` command fetches the data from the Virtual International Authority File (VIAF) and redirects the output into `viaf.xml`.

If you used the GUI, also use the `ls` command and confirm you know exactly what the name of the file is—your computer may have added an extension that's not visible in the GUI. Now type

```
chmod 755 myfile
```

The `chmod` command changes the properties of the file. Normally, you can only read and write to files you create. The command above lets you execute them like programs. Now type

```
./myfile
```

The program will run and an authority record from the VIAF that begins like the one shown in figure 8.1 appears in `viaf.xml`.

```
<?xml version="1.0" encoding="UTF-8"?>
<ns1:VIAFCluster xmlns="http://viaf.org/viaf/terms#"
xmlns:foaf="http://xmlns.com/foaf/0.1/" xmlns:owl="http://
www.w3.org/2002/07/owl#" xmlns:rdf="http://www.
w3.org/1999/02/22-rdf-syntax-ns#" xmlns:void="http://rdfs.
org/ns/void#" xmlns:ns1="http://viaf.org/viaf/terms#">
  <ns1:viafID>34791410</ns1:viafID>
  <ns1:Document about="http://viaf.org/viaf/34791410/">
    <ns1:inDataset resource="http://viaf.org/viaf/data"/>
    <ns1:primaryTopic resource="http://viaf.org/
viaf/34791410"/>
  </ns1:Document>
  <ns1:nameType>Personal</ns1:nameType>
[... content removed for brevity ...]
```

Figure 8.1: **Record retrieved from VIAF**

Type

```
cat viaf.xml
```

to verify the content is there. Now open the file containing the `curl` command and add the following lines:

```
# You can write notes in your code by preceding
# them with a hash mark to help remind you of
# what your code does
# retrieves a record from VIAF and sends it to viaf.xml
curl 'https://viaf.org/viaf/34791410/viaf.xml' > viaf.
    xml
echo 'Titles associated with record 34791410:'
# selects titles and prepends each line with 2 spaces
xmlstarlet sel -t -v "//ns1:title" -n viaf.xml |sed
    's/^/ /'
```

Now run `./myfile` again—the titles will appear in a list after the label.

In this three-line script, we retrieved a complex XML document from the internet, extracted information of interest, and printed it attractively to the screen.

Variables

Variables are names that you create to store data so you can access or modify it later. For example, let's rewrite the `myfile` script to use variables. Erase the existing information and add

```
rec_no="34791410"

# retrieves a record and stores it in $auth_record
# Notice how we use command substitution as described in
# Chapter 1 to capture the output of the curl command.
# The -s switch just makes it so it doesn't show a progress
meter
auth_record=$(curl -s "https://viaf.org/viaf/$rec_no/viaf.
xml")
# extracts author and stores it in $author
#
# Notice also how the backslash is used to distribute a long
command
# over two lines
author=$(echo $auth_record | xmlstarlet sel -t -v \ "//ns1:-
mainHeadings/ns1:data[position()=1]/ns1:text")

# extracts titles which are stored $titles
titles=$(echo $auth_record | xmlstarlet sel -t -v "//ns1:ti-
tle")
# counts titles and stores value in $num_titles
num_titles=$(echo "$titles" | wc -l)

echo "$num_titles titles are associated with record
$author:"
# prints titles after prepending each with 2 spaces
```

Figure 8.2: **Scripting with variables**

Although these changes made the script a little more complicated, they also made it more flexible. In just a few lines, we've downloaded the titles associated with an author, counted them, and listed the results in a nicely formatted display.

```
3 titles are associated with record Banerjee, Kyle.:
Building digital libraries a how-to-do-it manual
Digital libraries integrating content and systems
Migrating library data : a practical manual
```

In this book and elsewhere, you'll see variables referenced using different syntax. In some cases, this is a case of multiple syntaxes meaning the same thing. In others, the syntax is relevant.

If you're new to scripting, don't try to memorize the differences—they're nonintuitive and it's easier to look them up. That said, you should be aware that in general:

- Syntax for variables containing numbers is often different than syntax for variables containing strings—the wrong format could result in an error or much different behavior than you expect.
- Quotes are often important, especially if your variables contains whitespace characters. If you don't use quotes when a variable contains words and spaces, the command interpreter will mistake them for separate commands. Most of the data wrangling that librarians do involves strings, so you'll probably want to enclose your variables in straight double quotes most of the time.

Arguments

Sometimes you need a script that can accept input. For example, it's clunky to edit the myfile script shown in figure 8.2 every time you want to look up another author—it's much more convenient to pass the record number to the script as an argument so that to execute it, we'd type

```
./myfile 34791410
```

To do this, it's only necessary to make one small modification to the script—notice the first line in figure 8.3.

```
# $1 is the argument given to the script at the command
line. If more than one
# argument is given, they become $2, $3, $4, etc
rec_no="$1"

# Retrieves a record and stores it in $auth_record
# Notice how we use command substitution as described in
# Chapter 1 to capture the output of the curl command.
# The -s switch just makes it so it doesn't show a progress
```

```
meter
auth_record=$(curl -s "https://viaf.org/viaf/$rec_no/viaf.
xml")

# extracts author and stores it in $author
author=$(echo $auth_record | xmlstarlet sel -t -v \
"//ns1:mainHeadings/ns1:data[position()=1]/ns1:text")

# extracts titles which are stored $titles
titles=$(echo $auth_record | xmlstarlet sel -t -v "//ns1:ti-
tle")
# counts titles and stores value in $num_titles
num_titles=$(echo "$titles" | wc -l)

echo "$num_titles titles are associated with author $author"
```

Figure 8.3: **Scripts that accept arguments**

Notice that `rec_no` is defined as `$1` rather the number itself as it was in figure 8.1—that notation simply tells the script to use the input given to the script. If you want to pass more than one argument, the subsequent arguments are simply numbered, that is, the second argument is `$2`, the third argument is `$3`, and so on. Arguments are delimited by spaces, so if an individual argument needs to contain spaces, it must be surrounded by quotes.

Be aware that there are other ways for scripts to accept arguments from the command line. You can use your favorite web search engine for assistance when the above method doesn't suffice. For example, the simple method demonstrated here will not work if your script understands three arguments but the second one is sometimes missing—the script would think that the third value is the second. There are ways to do this, but the simple method shown in figure 8.2 will meet the vast majority of data wrangling needs.

Conditional Execution

Sometimes you'll need commands to execute only when certain criteria are met. For example, let's suppose we want our sample script to search VIAF only when it thinks the record number is valid and to give us a warning instead if a record number contains anything other than digits. Modifying the script as shown in figure 8.3 could achieve this.

```
rec_no="$1"
# We need to store the regular expression in a variable
# to get it to match properly within the conditional expres-
sion

regexp="^[0-9]+$"

# The double brackets tell the system to test for a condi-
tion

if [[ $rec_no =~ $regexp ]]; then
        auth_record=$(curl -s "https://viaf.org/viaf/$rec_
no/viaf.xml")
        author=$(echo $auth_record | xmlstarlet sel -t -v \
"//ns1:mainHeadings/ns1:data[position()=1]/ns1:text")
        titles=$(echo $auth_record | xmlstarlet sel -t -v \
"//ns1:title")
        num_titles=$(echo "$titles" | wc -l)
        echo "$num_titles titles are associated with author
$author"
else
   echo "$rec_no does not appear to be a valid record number"
fi
```

Figure 8.4: **Script containing conditional statement**

Try running the file with a valid number

./myfile 34791410

and an invalid one

./myfile X4791410

to verify that it works. Notice the bracket notation as well as the fact that the regular expression is outside the conditional statement—this is necessary for regular expressions but not for other strings and numbers.

Be aware that different operators are used for integers rather than strings as shown in figure 8.5:

Comparison Operator	String	Integer
Equal to	==	-eq
Not equal to	!=	-ne
Greater than	>	-gt
Greater than or equal to	>=	-ge
Less than	<	-lt
Less than or equal to	<=	-le

Figure 8.5: **Scripting comparison operators**

Loops

One of the major purposes of automation is to eliminate repetitive tasks, so loops play an important role in scripting. You may need to perform some operation on a large group of files or every record within a file or to perform a series of related operations on an individual element. If a loop were added to the script in figure 8.4, it could look up an entire file of records rather than just one.

The nature of loops is they operate while some condition is met. For purposes of data wrangling, loops take two forms:

1. They iterate through every item in a list in the form:

```
for some_variable in <list>
do
    <something>
done
```

2. They perform a test in the form

```
while [perform some test]
do
    <something>
done
```

To understand the difference between these two forms, create a file named "rec_nos" containing the following numbers:

```
34791410
96994048
116796842
104023256
95155403
```

Also, make sure you have a file containing the code in figure 8.4 in `myfile`. Now type

```
for number in $(cat rec_nos);do ./myfile $number;done
```

at the command line. The result will be similar to what appears in figure 8.6.

```
banerjek@BICB242: ~/Desktop                                          —  □  ×
banerjek@BICB242:~/Desktop$ for number in $(cat rec_nos);do ./myfile $number;done
3 titles are associated with author Banerjee, Kyle.
437 titles are associated with author Shakespeare, William, 1564-1616.
54 titles are associated with author Rowling, J.K., 1965-
101 titles are associated with author Dostoyevsky, Fyodor, 1821-1881
99 titles are associated with author Orwell, George, 1903-1950.
banerjek@BICB242:~/Desktop$
```

Figure 8.6: **Using loops from the command line**

In this example, the command `cat rec_nos` returns the list of numbers in the file. Within the loop, the value of $number is individually set to each one and sent to the script. This sort of loop is very useful for performing tasks such as processing lists within files—or even lists of files themselves obtained from the ls or find commands.

This same loop structure can be put in a script with newlines substituted for the semicolons to help make it more readable, that is,

```
for number in $(cat rec_nos)
do
./myfile $number
done
```

To experiment with the second form of loop, notice the construction of the script in figure 8.7:

```
filename="$1"

regexp="^[0-9]+$"
recs_processed=0

while read rec_no
do
    if [[ $rec_no =~ $regexp ]]; then
        auth_record=$(curl -s "https://viaf.org/viaf/$rec_no/
            viaf.xml")
        author=$(echo $auth_record | xmlstarlet sel -t -v \
            "//ns1:mainHeadings/ns1:data[position()=1]/ns1:
                text")
        titles=$(echo $auth_record | xmlstarlet sel -t -v "//
            ns1:title")
        num_titles=$(echo "$titles" | wc -l)
```

```
        echo "$num_titles titles are associated with author
            $author"
        $recs_processed
    else
        echo "$rec_no does not appear to be a valid record
            number"
        continue
    fi

done <$filename

echo "All instructions have been executed"
```

Figure 8.7: **Script that uses a loop to read a file**

In figure 8.7, instructions within the loop are executed only while lines can be read from the file. If the entry looks like a valid record number, the script attempts to process it; otherwise, it prints a message to the screen.

Sometimes you might want to break out of a loop entirely or simply skip to the next iteration. Notice the code in figure 8.8—if x equals 3, the program prints a message, adds two, and returns to the beginning of the loop without adding one as it does for all other values. Also notice that even though the counter in the while statement goes to 10, the program stops when x equals 8—the break statement takes it completely out of the loop. Figure 8.9 shows the actual output from running the code.

```
x=0
while [ $x -lt 10 ]
do
        if [ $x -eq 3 ];then
                echo "Not printing this entry, skipping to
                    next iteration"
                let x=x+2
                continue
        elif [ $x -eq 8 ];then
                echo "Breaking the loop early at x=$x"
                break
        else
                echo "x=$x"
        fi

        let x=x+1
done
```

Figure 8.8: **Code example of loops with continues and breaks**

```
banerjek@BICB242: ~/Desktop                                              —   □   ×
banerjek@BICB242:~/Desktop$ cat looptest
x=0
while [ $x -lt 10 ]
do
  if [ $x -eq 3 ];then
    echo "Not printing this entry, skipping to next iteration"
    let x=x+2
    continue
  elif [ $x -eq 8 ];then
    echo "Breaking the loop early at x=$x"
    break
  else
    echo "x=$x"
  fi

  let x=x+1
done

banerjek@BICB242:~/Desktop$ ./looptest
x=0
x=1
x=2
Not printing this entry, skipping to next iteration
x=5
x=6
x=7
Breaking the loop early at x=8
banerjek@BICB242:~/Desktop$
```

Figure 8.9: **Executing a loop containing continues and breaks**

A little bit of scripting knowledge goes a long way. If you know a few utilities, how to redirect output from commands to file and other commands, store information in variables, make conditional statements, and set up loops, there's very little you can't do.

## CHAPTER 9

Solving Common Problems

I f you've made it this far, you already know what you need to work with a wide range of data wrangling challenges. However, some are common enough that it's worth addressing specifically.

Viewing Large Files

The easiest way to understand a file is by looking at it. You might need to know how it's structured or how data has been entered. You may want to examine the quality and consistency of the data, or perhaps you're getting a message that there is an error in the data on a particular line or at a particular character position.

For most people, the first instinct is to look at the file in a text editor. But what if the file is 100 MB or 10 GB? The good news is that viewing data in huge files is both fast and easy, even on a regular laptop whether you simply want to browse through the file, examine specific data, or inspect specific locations in the file.

If you just want to look at the file one page at a time, simply type

```
less myfile
```

Hit the spacebar to move forward through the file, "b" to move backwards through it, and "q" to quit. To search for text within the file simply hit a forward slash followed by a regular expression.

Locating Files That Contain Particular Data

To identify files containing specific data in the current directory and subdirectories containing specific data

```
grep -R "myregularexpression" *
```

identifies all filenames and lines containing a myregularexpression

```
grep -iR "myregularexpression" *
```

(notice -i option) performs a case insensitive search, and

```
grep -lR "myregularexpression" *
```

(notice -l option) only prints the filename.

Finding Files with Specific Characteristics

To locate all PDF files in the current directory and subdirectories modified in the past week:

```
find . -name '*.pdf' -mtime 7
```

To identify all files in the current directory and subdirectories greater than 10 MB and less than 100 MB

```
find . -size +10M -size -100M
```

To delete all tmp files in the current directory and subdirectories, and request confirmation for each delete individually

```
find . -name '.tmp' -exec rm -i {} \;
```

Note that any command can follow the exec parameter and the braces refer to the files found. For example, to copy all PDF files modified in the past week to the /pdf directory,

```
find . -name '*.pdf' -mtime 7 -exec cp {} /pdf \;
```

(notice -l option) only prints the filename.

Working with Internal Metadata

Internal metadata is stored within files themselves rather than separately, but most files that you work with that are not plain text contain internal metadata. Librarians rarely modify internal metadata because it is seen as modifying the file and it does change checksums even though the actual images, documents, videos, and so on are unchanged.

It may be necessary to read or modify internal metadata for a number of reasons, including:

- You want to identify all photos in a directory that are higher or lower than a certain resolution.
- You don't want inaccurate metadata being transmitted with the file.

- You are migrating into a new system, and the new system gets metadata from the file rather than a separate data file.

To read and modify internal metadata, you need `exiftool`.

To install on the `linux` command line within windows:

```
sudo apt-get install exiftool
```

and on MacOS

```
brew install exiftool
```

A good list of `exiftool` examples provided by the developer can be found at https://owl.phy.queensu.ca/~phil/exiftool/examples.html.

`Exiftool` has powerful capabilities involving reading, creating, and internal metadata. It has flexible and customizable output options. Consult the documentation at https://www.sno.phy.queensu.ca/~phil/exiftool/exiftool_pod.html for more information.

For example, to list the names, pixel dimensions, and file sizes of all files in the current directory and subdirectories in tab delimited format

```
exiftool -r -T -FileName -ImageSize -FileSize *
```

Sample output:

```
P9291917.JPG 1200x1600 530 kB
P9292014.JPG 1920x1440 613 kB
PA131316.JPG 4608x3456 3.6 MB
```

To see all the metadata associated with a single file

```
exiftool filename
```

Example output:

```
File Name : P9291917.JPG
Directory : .
File Size : 530 kB
File Modification Date/Time : 2018:09:30 07:12:26-07:00
File Access Date/Time : 2018:09:30 07:12:26-07:00
File Inode Change Date/Time : 2018:10:03 07:53:01-07:00
File Permissions : rwxrwxrwx
File Type : JPEG
File Type Extension : jpg
MIME Type : image/jpeg
JFIF Version : 1.01
Exif Byte Order : Big-endian (Motorola, MM)
Processing Software : Windows Photo Editor
    10.0.10011.16384
```

```
Image Description : OLYMPUS DIGITAL CAMERA
Make : OLYMPUS CORPORATION
Camera Model Name : TG-4
Orientation : Horizontal (normal)
X Resolution : 314
Y Resolution : 314
ISO : 100
Sensitivity Type : Standard Output Sensitivity
Exif Version : 0230
Date/Time Original : 2018:09:29 10:33:21
Create Date : 2018:09:29 10:33:21
Components Configuration : Y, Cb, Cr, -
Exposure Compensation : 0
Max Aperture Value : 2.8
Crop Width : 4608
Crop Height : 3456
Sensor Calibration : 4095 610
Noise Reduction 2 : (none)
Distortion Correction 2 : Off
Shading Compensation 2 : On
Multiple Exposure Mode : Off; 1
Aspect Ratio : 4:3
[ . . . extensive technical data omitted for brevity . . . ]
```

Working with APIs

An API is a software interface that makes it easier to talk to other software. Most nonprogrammers find the concept of an API intimidating, largely because of the jargon surrounding them—but they're really quite simple. Integrated library systems, institutional repositories, and other systems often offer a REST (REpresentational State Transfer) API. In plain English, this means that they work the way web forms have worked since the early 1990s. As a matter of fact, you can even use a web browser to interact with many APIs.

With REST APIs, you read data using an HTTP (HyperText Transport Protocol) GET command the same way you would with a web page. In the background, your browser literally sends the word GET along with what it's requesting. To add data, you use the HTTP POST command (your browser literally sends the word POST in the background when you submit many web forms).

In other words, when a system has a REST API, all it means is that you can use ordinary web protocols to interact with it. You can interact REST APIs using any modern programming language, and it's simple enough that people with no coding experience can learn to do this in a few minutes.

If you'd like to experiment with an API right away, the Digital Public Library of America (DPLA) is a good place to start—just follow the instructions at https://pro.dp.la/developers/api-codex. The idea of using an API to download and analyze a series of records sounds intimidating, but it's surprisingly easy even if you're still confused about what an API is.

However, that API only allows you to read data, so we're going to use a more sophisticated example—namely to use the DataCite API to update the metadata associated with a DOI. Retrieving the metadata associated with a DOI is a simple one-line command.

```
curl -s --user "username:password" "https://mds.datacite
    .org/metadata/10.6083/fp65-8k33"
```

As is the case with DataCite, the DPLA API also lets you conduct a search with a single line—so you can see how easy using an API can be!

The response to the command above from DataCite is shown in figure 9.1.

```
<?xml version="1.0" encoding="UTF-8"?>
<resource xmlns:xsi="http://www.w3.org/2001/XMLSche-
ma-instance" xmlns="http://datacite.org/schema/kernel-4"
xsi:schemaLocation="http://datacite.org/schema/kernel-4
http://schema.datacite.org/meta/kernel-4/metadata.xsd">
  <identifier identifierType="DOI">10.6083/FP65-8K33
      </identifier>
  <creators>
    <creator>
      <creatorName>Banerjee, Kyle</creatorName>
      <givenName>Kyle</givenName>
      <familyName>Banerjee</familyName>
    </creator>
  </creators>
  <titles>
    <title>Building Digital Libraries</title>
  </titles>
  <publisher>ALA Neal Schuman</publisher>
  <publicationYear>2019</publicationYear>
  <resourceType resourceTypeGeneral="Text">CreativeWork
      </resourceType>
  <dates>
    <date dateType="Issued">2019</date>
  </dates>
  <version/>
</resource>
```

Figure 9.1: **Response from DataCite API for DOI**

Let's suppose we wanted to update that DOI by adding the coauthor. Figure 9.2 shows a script that would accomplish this. Notice that backslashes have been used to break long lines into multiple lines.

```
# store authorization credentials in a file and load them
into a variable

AUTH=$(cat auth)
SERVICE="https://mds.datacite.org/metadata"
DOI="10.6083/fp65-8k33"

# retrieve metadata from DataCite and store in XMLDOC

XMLDOC=$(curl -s --user "$AUTH"  "$SERVICE/$DOI")

# xmlstarlet is picky about namespaces, so we strip the info
# out for now

XMLDOC=$(echo $XMLDOC | xmlstarlet fo | sed 's/^<resource
.*$/<resource>/')

# add a creator in the creators hierarchy. Notice the
[not(...)] XPath notation. Otherwise
# the element would be created everywhere the path matches.
We only want it to be
# in the new (i.e. empty) element

XMLDOC=$(echo $XMLDOC |xmlstarlet ed -s /resource/creators
-t elem -n creator \
-s '/resource/creators/creator[not(creatorName)]' -t elem -n
creatorName -v "Reese, Terry" \
-s '/resource/creators/creator[not(givenName)]' -t elem -n
givenName -v "Terry" \
-s '/resource/creators/creator[not(familyName)]' -t elem -n
familyName -v "Reese")

# adds back the namespace information we stripped out

XMLDOC=$(echo $XMLDOC |xmlstarlet ed -d '/resource/@*' -s '/
resource' -t attr \
-n xmlns -v "http://datacite.org/schema/kernel-4" -s '/
resource' -t attr \
-n "xmlns:xsi" -v "http://www.w3.org/2001/XMLSchema-in-
stance" -s '/resource' -t attr \
-n "xsi:schemaLocation" -v "http://datacite.org/schema/ker-
nel-4 \
```

```
http://schema.datacite.org/meta/kernel-4/metadata.xsd")

# Send the updated XML document back to DataCite
curl -H "Content-Type:application/xml;charset=UTF-8"  X POST
-i --user "$AUTH" \
-d "$XMLDOC" $SERVICE
```

Figure 9.2: **Script to add creator using DataCite API**

The script looks intimidating, but all that is really happening is

1. The `curl` command retrieves the metadata that is stored in XMLDOC.
2. `xmlstarlet` adds a creator element, and within that adds creatorName, givenName, and familyName—that is, four elements are added in one command!
3. curl is used to put the data back.

And that's it! After that simple script was run, figure 9.3 shows us that the record was updated in DataCite. The commands used to strip out and add the namespace information back make this example look more complex than it is. However, these commands were necessary because XMLStarlet is picky about namespaces, and the easiest way to handle that was to simply remove them temporarily.

```
<?xml version="1.0" encoding="UTF-8"?>
<resource xmlns="http://datacite.org/schema/kernel-4"
xmlns:xsi="http://www.w3.org/2001/XMLSchema-instance"
xsi:schemaLocation="http://datacite.org/schema/kernel-4
http://schema.datacite.org/meta/kernel-4/metadata.xsd">
  <identifier identifierType="DOI">10.6083/FP65-8K33
    </identifier>
  <creators>
    <creator>
      <creatorName>Banerjee, Kyle</creatorName>
      <givenName>Kyle</givenName>
      <familyName>Banerjee</familyName>
    </creator>
    <creator>
      <creatorName>Reese, Terry</creatorName>
      <givenName>Terry</givenName>
      <familyName>Reese</familyName>
    </creator>
  </creators>
  <titles>
```

```
   <title>Building Digital Libraries</title>
</titles>   <publisher>ALA Neal Schuman</publisher>
<publicationYear>2019</publicationYear>
<resourceType resourceTypeGeneral="Text">CreativeWork
   </resourceType>
<dates>
   <date dateType="Issued">2019</date>
</dates>
<version/>
</resource>
```

Figure 9.3: **Response from DataCite API for DOI after updating creator**

Combining Data from Different Sources

Librarians sometimes have to combine data from multiple files into a single file. For example, suppose you're thinking of buying a new journal or e-book package and you're wondering which titles overlap with what you already have, but you also want those that don't overlap to determine how many quality resources you're potentially adding. Fortunately, there's a built-in command that makes this easy, namely join.

Let's suppose you have the list of ISBNs below listing your current holdings in a file named isbns.

```
9780838916353
083891635X
9780838917237
9780838917244
9780838917237
9780838915035
9780838917145
```

and a list of ISBNs and titles from the prospective package in a tab delimited file named titles.

```
9781783302260        Records Information and Data
9781783302604        Data Organization
9780838917237        Building Digital Libraries
9781783300983        The Data Librarian's Handbook
9780838915035        Migrating Library Data
```

join is a simple command to use, but it requires files to be sorted before they are combined.

```
sort isbns > isbns_sorted
sort titles> titles_sorted
```

Now the `join` can be performed.

```
join isbns_sorted titles_sorted
9780838915035          Migrating Library Data
978083891723           Building Digital Libraries
978083891723           Building Digital Libraries
```

The example here is simple and could have easily been handled by Excel. However, the `join` command works very quickly on files of any size—even millions of lines. Moreover, in real world situations, the data you're working with will typically be dirty. For example, the ISBNs might not be formatted consistently (some might have hyphens or qualifying information while others don't, there could be multiple numbers on lines, etc.). But these can be fixed quickly using `sed` or some other utility making the command line option much faster and easier than alternatives.

One thing to be aware of when using `join` with text is that some characters will cause `join` to complain that files aren't sorted even though they have been. This can be caused because `join` is picky about how mixed-case data are sorted and by internationalization settings on your system. If you get this error on files you know to be sorted, then just resort each file as demonstrated below:

```
LC_COLLATE=C sort file1 > sorted_file1
LC_COLLATE=C sort file2 > sorted_file2
```

and then join the file as shown below

```
LANG=en_EN join sorted_file1 sorted_file2
```

Other Tasks

There are far more tasks specific to individual situations that you might be called upon to perform as a data wrangler than can be described in a short handbook. You might need to convert file formats, extract text from images, or perform any number of functions. The important thing to be aware of is that specialized utilities are available to perform most tasks. For example, `image-magick` is excellent for converting image formats, `ffmpeg` is great for video, `pdftotext` is excellent for extracting text from PDFs, and there are countless other useful programs. In other words, when you don't know how to do something, it's a good idea to see if someone hasn't already provided an easy way to do it.

## CHAPTER 10

Conclusions

As you've seen in the previous chapters, you only need a little time to learn to do amazing things with a handful of commands. Although the syntax for some of the commands shown here is sometimes non-intuitive and intimidating, performing complex operations on large amounts of data is much easier than most people imagine

If you are new to data wrangling, the most important things to remember from this book are

1. **Most formats that librarians work with are ultimately text.** This means you can use the same basic tools and techniques with virtually any data file of any size. Often format specific tools are often not necessary.

2. **Powerful programs designed to do what you need** are already on the computer you use and can be accessed via the command line.

3. **You don't need a technical background to use the command line.** The reason the command line is powerful is because others have already written what you require—that's why you can do so much work with a single command.

4. **You can send the output of any command line program to any other command or program.** This allows you to combine the functionality of many specialized programs to do exactly what you require. The basic methods you will use most often are:

   - **Pipes**—Make the output of one program the input of another.
   - **Command substitution**—Make the output of one program the argument for another. When you want each line of output to be used as a separate input rather than all the output to be used as a single input, the `xargs` utility is useful for this.

5. **Complicated problems can be solved by breaking them into a series of simple steps and by simplifying the data itself.** Convert your data

into a format that will make it easiest to work with. Normalize capitalization, punctuation, whitespace, and anything else that will make life easier.

6. **You can write scripts that can do virtually anything with a simple text editor.** Scripts often just contain a sequence of commands, but they make it easy to run commands only when certain conditions are met.

7. **Regular expressions are powerful and support for them is built into many programs, including mainstream tools such as Microsoft Word.** Regular expressions are indispensable for data wrangling because they make it possible to perform sophisticated searches and replacements in just a few characters.

8. **A few tools are particularly handy for data wrangling. They are:**

   - grep—Possibly the most important data analysis tool, grep allows you to figure out what your data does and does not contain.
   - sed and tr—Allows you to perform complex modification of huge files easily and quickly. tr is excellent for eliminating or transforming problem characters and normalizing case.
   - awk—Allows you to perform complex database-like operations on fielded data.
   - paste and join—Combine files.
   - sort—Sort data however you require.
   - uniq—Identify/remove duplicates and count occurrences.
   - jq—Select, filter, and format JSON data.
   - xmlstarlet—Select, filter, and manipulate XML documents.
   - curl—Interact with APIs and retrieve data over a network.

People like to do things the easy way because it's inevitably more fun and efficient. As such, they often avoid the unfamiliar, which presents unknown challenges. Although this behavior is both rational and understandable, it also sometimes causes them to do things the hard way—or think they lack the skills or tools to do what they need—simply because they've never had a chance to familiarize themselves with alternative methods and tools.

As overwhelming as some commands in this book may seem, they represent only a tiny fraction of the total available—many more that perform an incredible variety of tasks are available. The ones selected for this book were chosen because they have proven particularly useful for purposes of wrangling data in a library environment. On a similar note, only a small portion of the functionality of the commands discussed here has been discussed. Entire books have been written on many of these commands and simply listing (without even describing) the options (switches) that can be used to modify their behavior would take pages. This detail has been intentionally omitted to help you focus on functionality that benefits you most. When you find yourself wishing there were a command that performs a function or that a command behaved differently than it does, you should consult other resources to see if the functionality you desire already exists because it very well might.

If you're interested in learning more about using the command line, the best approach is usually to investigate how people approach specific tasks you're interested in performing. Don't try to memorize commands or methods because it's virtually impossible to retain the detail. Instead, just get a sense of what's possible and look up what you need when you need it.

That also applies to the contents of this book. For example, if you don't work with JSON and don't need to communicate with other machines, don't worry about learning about `jq` and `curl`. Rather, just be aware that simple commands exist for working with JSON and getting machines to communicate. Don't worry about the other sections that talk about things you don't work with—if you have to work with these things later, you can look up the details even if you've forgotten the names of the commands.

Don't be shy about getting help when you can't get something to work. For example, let's suppose you need to match a multiline expression with `sed` or `grep`, but didn't remember from chapter 2 that those two commands can't match newline characters—even if they're great at matching everything else—because they process data one line at a time. Just type, "why can't I match newline characters with sed" into your favorite search engine and you'll have the answer fast. It's virtually guaranteed that many people have experienced the same issue and it's been discussed extensively.

Make sure that your needs—not your tools—drive your process. In other words, the question should always be, "how should I do X?" rather than "how do I use this tool to do X?" even if solutions utilizing familiar tools are preferred. Otherwise, there's a tendency to redefine the need in terms that the tool is designed to solve. For example, even though `sed` is not designed to match newlines, it is possible use it to replace them. This line would do the trick:

```
sed -e ':a' -e 'N' -e '$!ba' -e 's/\n/ /g' myfile
```

This is incredibly awkward because you're trying to match something sed is designed not to match. Although there are multiple ways to do things and what's "best" depends on circumstances, it's important to recognize when you're trying to use the wrong tool for the job.

The advantage of the commands presented in this book is that they're useful in a wide variety of situations. At the same time, be ready to learn something new if you feel like you're doing things the hard way. As the old adage goes, when you have a hammer in your hand, every problem looks like a nail. Screws look like nails and you can drive them in with a hammer. But just because you can doesn't make it a good idea.

If you've made it this far, you know what you need to do serious data wrangling. You know that for all the fancy jargon surrounding data, it's mostly text. You can perform complex analysis and manipulation of files containing millions of lines using a small number of simple tools that are already on your laptop. You know how to automate processes with a simple text editor. And possibly most importantly, now that you know how easy it is, you can have more fun helping others with data.

One-Line Wonders

The command line is powerful, but the syntax is often confusing. The following commands and functions are likely to be especially useful in a library context. They have been organized into seven categories:

1. Locating, viewing, and performing basic file operations
2. Retrieving and sending information over a network
3. Sorting, counting, deduplication, and file comparison
4. Transforming text
5. Useful scripting operations (assumes the most commonly used interpreter), so alternate syntax is necessary in some environments
6. Working with delimited files
7. Working with JSON and XML

Each example addresses a specific problem—you may notice that many utilize command line switches not discussed in other sections of this book. Discussing the full functionality of the commands presented in this book would result in an overwhelming amount of detail because simply enumerating the options with which they can be used could take many pages. When you find yourself wishing that a command had a specific capability not addressed here, you are encouraged to consult your favorite search engine or online forum to learn more because there's an excellent chance that someone has already developed an elegant solution to your problem.

Locating, Viewing, and Performing Basic File Operations

Combine Information from Multiple Files into a Single File
```
cat file1 file2 file3 file4 file5 > combinedfile
```

Combine Three Files, Each Consisting of a Single Column, into a Three-Column Table
```
paste file1 file2 file3 > 3columnfile
```

Extract 1,000 Random Lines or Records from a File
```
shuf file.txt | head -n 10
```

FIND FILES WITH SPECIFIC CHARACTERISTICS

To locate all PDF files in the current directory and subdirectories modified in the past week:
```
find . -name '*.pdf' -mtime 7
```

To identify all files in the current directory and subdirectories greater than 10 MB and less than 100 MB
```
find . -size +10M -size -100M
```

To delete all tmp files in the current directory and subdirectories, requesting confirmation for each delete individually
```
find . -name '.tmp' -exec rm -i {} \;
```

Note that any command can follow the exec parameter and the braces refer to the files found. For example, to copy all PDF files modified in the past week to the /pdf directory,
```
find . -name '*.pdf' -mtime 7 -exec cp {} /pdf \;
```

Find All Lines in All Files in the Current Directory as Well as All Subdirectories Containing a Regular Expression
```
grep -R "myregularexpression" *
```

Identify All Files in Current Directories and Subdirectories That Contain a Value
```
grep -lR 'myregularexpression' *
```

List All Files in Current Directory and Subdirectories over a 100 MB in Order of Decreasing Size

```
find . -type f -size +100M | xargs ls -1 | sort -k5nr
```

`find . -type f +100M`	Find all files in current directory hierarchy over 100 MB.
`xargs`	Convert each line output from previous command to argument for next command.
`ls -1`	List all file attributes of each file provided via `xargs`.
`sort -k5nr`	Sorts list of files in order of descending filesize. `-k5` indicates the fifth field (field containing size), `n` indicates numeric rather than character sort, and `r` indicates reverse sort.

List the Names, Pixel Dimensions, and File Sizes of All Files in the Current Directory and Subdirectories in Tab Delimited Format

```
exiftool -r -T -FileName -ImageSize -FileSize *
```

Print Line Number of File That Match Occurred On

```
cat myfile | grep -n "pattern_to_match"
```

Split Large Files into Smaller Chunks with Each File Breaking on a Line

(Split into 1,000 chunks)
```
split --number=l/1000 largefile
```

(Split into 1 GB chunks)
```
split --line-bytes=1GB largefile
```

View 200 Characters Starting at Position 385621 in a File

```
cat myfile | tail -c +385621 | head -c 200
```

View Lines 4369–4374 of a File

```
sed -n 4369,4374p myfile
```

Retrieving and Sending Information over a Network

Retrieve a Document from the Web and Send It to a File

```
curl 'https://interestingsite.org/document.xml' >
   myfile.xml
```

Send an XML Document to an API Requiring HTTP Authentication

```
curl -H "Content-Type:application/xml;charset=UTF-8" -X
   POST -i \
--user "credentials" -d @myfile.xml http://site.org/api
```

Sorting, Counting, Deduplication, and File Comparison

Combine Two Files on a Common Field

```
join file file2 > combined_file
```

Join is picky about how files are sorted. If join gives you errors saying the files aren't sorted, use the following commands.

```
LC_COLLATE=C sort file1 > sorted_file1
LC_COLLATE=C sort file2 > sorted_file2
```

and then join the file as shown below

```
LANG=en_EN join sorted_file1 sorted_file2
```

Compare Two Sorted Files

`comm -23 File1 File2`	Show lines unique to `File1`.
`comm -13 File1 File2`	Show lines unique to `File2`.
`comm -12 File1 File2`	Show lines common to `File1` and `File2`.

Count Occurrences for Each Entry in a File, Listed in Order of Decreasing Frequency

```
sort myfile | uniq -c | sort -k1nr
```

Count Records Containing an Expression

```
cat myfile | grep "expression" | wc -1
```

Count Words, Lines, and Characters in File

`wc -w myfile`	Count words in `myfile`.
`wc -1 myfile`	Count lines in `myfile`.
`wc -m myfile`	Count characters in `myfile`.

Identify All Unique Entries and Supply a Count of How Many Times Each Occurs

```
sort myfile | uniq -c
```

Sort a File and Remove Duplicates, Show Only Duplicated Entries, or Show Only Unique Entries

`sort -u myfile`	Remove all duplicates.
`sort myfile	uniq -d`	Show only entries that are duplicated.
`sort myfile	uniq -u`	Show only values that are unique (i.e., not duplicated).

Useful Scripting Operations

Capture Parameters Passed to a Script

```
first_parameter=$1
second_parameter=$2
third_parameter=$3
```

Divide a Line into Parameters

```
line="term1 term2 term3"
params=($line)
echo ${params[0]} ➞ "term1"
echo ${params[1]} ➞ "term2"
echo ${params[2]} ➞ "term3"
```

Iterate through Every Item in Parameter List

The code below

```
for param in parms
do
    echo $param
done
```

would result in:

```
term1
term2
term3
```

Perform a Loop

```
while [perform some test]
do
mycommands
done
```

Perform an Operation Conditionally

```
if [[ $myvar =~ $regexp ]]; then
echo "regular expression found"
else
echo "regular expression failed"
fi

cat myfile | ./myscript
```

Run a Script on Every Line of a File

```
for each_line in $(cat myfile);do ./myscript $each_
    line;done
```

Send the Output of a Command as Arguments to Another Command

```
firstcommand | xargs secondcommand
```

Send the Output of a Command to Another Command

```
firstcommand | secondcommand
```

Send the Output of a Command to a File

```
mycommand > myfile
```

Store the Output of a Command in a Variable

```
myvar=$(mycommand)
```

Use Foreign Character Sets in a Terminal Window

```
locale-gen en_US.UTF-8
```

Transforming Text

Convert File of Dates to YYYY-MM-DD Format

```
cat myfile | while read line; do date -d "$line"
    "+%Y-%m-%d"; done
```

cat myfile	Prints out myfile.
| while read line	Send output to "while" construct, which stores each line in the $line variable.
Do	Do everything that follows until reaching the "done" construct as long as the conditions of the "while" construct (namely being able to read lines) are met.
date -d "$line" "+%Y-%m-%d"	Convert the value stored in $line to YYYY-MM-DD.

Convert to Title Case

```
cat mytest.txt | sed 's/[^ ]\+/\L\u&/g'
```

cat mytest.txt	Prints out mytext.txt.
| sed	Send output to stream editor. Everything in search expression will be replaced by replacement expression, both of which are delimited by forward slashes.
[^]\+	One or more characters that aren't spaces.
\L	Turn replacement to lowercase until \u or \e is found.
\u	Turn next character to upper case.
&	Entire string found in search expression.
G	Global—keep searching even after finding a match.

Convert to Upper Case

```
cat myfile | tr '[:lower:]' '[:upper:]'
```

Convert List of Names from Direct Order to Indirect Order

```
cat names | sed 's/^\([a-zA-Z0-9 \.\-]*\) \(.*\)/\2,
    \1/'
```

`cat names`	Prints out names.
`| sed`	Send output to stream editor. Everything in search expression will be replaced by replacement expression, both of which are delimited by forward slashes.
`^\(`	From beginning of line, capture all alphanumeric characters, periods, and hyphens until `\)` is reached and store it in `\1`.
`\(.*\)`	Store the rest of the line in `\2`.
`\2, \1`	Print `\2` followed by a comma and a space by `\1`, effectively inverting the names.

Extract and Manipulate All Lines in a File That Match a Complex Pattern

`sed 's/search_for/replace_ with/' myfile`	Print `myfile` to screen while replacing `search_for` with `replace_with`.
`sed -i 's/search_for/replace_ with/' myfile`	Modify `myfile`, replacing `search_ for` with `replace_with`.

Extract and Manipulate All Entries in All Files in an Entire Directory Hierarchy That Match a Pattern

```
find . -type f | xargs sed -i 's/search_for/replace_
    with/'
```

`find . -type f`	Identify all files from present directory (to identify directories only, use `type d`).
`|xargs`	Use file list from previous commands are arguments for whatever follows `xargs`.
`sed -i 's/search_for/ replace_with/' myfile`	Modify `myfile`, replacing `search_for` with `replace_with`.

Remove Lines from a File That Match a Pattern

```
sed -i '/pattern_to_match/d' myfile
```

Remove Carriage Return Characters Inserted by Windows Programs from a File

```
cat myfile | tr -d '\r'
```

Remove Newline Characters from a File

```
cat myfile | tr -d '\n'
```

Replace Newlines in a File with Character 7 (Bell)

```
cat myfile | tr '\n' '\007'
```

Replace Search_Expr with Replace_Expr Only on Lines That Contain Condition_Expr

```
sed -i '/condition_expr/s/search_expr/replace_expr/g'
    myfile
```

Replace Search_Expr with Replace_Expr Except on Lines that Contain Condition_Expr

```
sed -i '/condition_expr/!s/search_expr/replace_expr/g'
    myfile
```

Replace Smart Quotes with Straight Quotes

```
sed -i 's/\x93/"/g' myfile (left double quote)
sed -i 's/\x94/"/g' myfile (right double quote)
sed -i "s/\x91/'/g" myfile (left single quote)
sed -i "s/\x92/'/g" myfile (right single quote)
```

Working with Delimited Files

Convert Comma Delimited File Where Some Values Are Quoted and Some Values Are Not to Tab Delimited

```
these,values,aren't,quoted
0,"first line, second column",2.0,3
4.5,"second column of second line",6,7.2

cat csvfile | sed 's/\(([a-z0-9]*\)""*,"*\
    ([a-z0-9]*\)/\1\t\2/ig' > tab_delimited_file

these values aren't quoted
0 first line second column 2.0 3
4.5 second column of second line 6 7.2
```

This solution presumes fields begin and end with letters or numbers. The regular expression would have to be expanded if support for other characters were needed.

Convert Multiline Records to Table

Number of commas following `-d` should correspond with one less than number of fields per record. If there are four fields spread over four lines, then use three commas

```
Record1Field1
Record1Field2
Record1Field3
Record1Field4
Record2Field1
Record2Field2
Record2Field3
Record2Field4
paste -d",,,\n" -s myfile
Record1Field1,Record1Field2,Record1Field3,Record1Field4
Record2Field1,Record2Field2,Record2Field3,Record2Field4
```

`-d` indicates the delimiter being used so if tab delimited output is desired, the command would be

```
paste -d"\n\t\t\t" -s myfile
```

`-s` indicates that data should be pasted in serial—that is, horizontal rather than vertical fashion

Extract Individual Fields from Files

`cut -f3 myfile`	Extract third field from tab delimited file.
`cut -d "|" -f3`	Extracts the third field from pipe delimited file.

Find the Most Common Values in the Second Field of a File

```
cat file.txt | cut -f2 | sort | uniq -c | sort -k1nr | head
```

`cat file.txt`	Prints out file.txt.
`cut -f2`	Extracts the second field.
`Sort`	Sorts the headings.
`uniq -c`	Lists each heading with the number of occurrences of each heading.
`sort -k1nr`	Sorts list of headings in descending order by number of occurrences. `-k1` indicates the first field (field containing count), `n` indicates numeric rather than character sort, and `r` indicates reverse sort.
`Head`	Displays first ten lines of output (10 most used headings).

Find All Lines in Tab Delimited File Not Containing Six Fields

```
awk -F "\t" 'NF!=6' < myfile
```

Fix Delimited File That Contains Line Breaks in Fields

Solution presumes last field is terminated by quotes. If reliable pattern for end of last field is not a quote, replace the double quote in front of the first dollar sign with an appropriate regular expression.

```
awk -F "\t" '/"$/ {print;next;} {printf("%s",$0);}'
    myfile.txt
```

Remove Trailing and Leading Whitespace from Tab Delimited Data Fields

```
column -t myfile
```

Reorder Fields in a Tab Delimited File

Presuming a five-column file where you want to print the first, fifth, and third fields with a hyphen connecting the fifth and third fields,

```
cat myfile | awk 'BEGIN {FS="\t";OFS="\t"}{print $1,
    $5"-"$3}'
```

Working with JSON and XML

Add an Attribute to an XML Document

```
cat myfile.xml | xmlstarlet ed -a -s '/path_to_element'
    -t attr -n new_attribute -v 'New value'
```

Add an Element to an XML Document

```
cat myfile.xml | xmlstarlet ed -a -s '/path_to_new
    _element[not(new_element)]' -t elem -n new_element
    -v 'New value'
```

Apply XSLT Stylesheet to XML Document

```
xmlstarlet tr mystylesheet.xsl -n myfile.xml
```

Convert JSON to Tab Delimited Format

```
cat myfile.json | jq -r '[.element1, .element2,
    .element3] | @tsv'
```

Delete Elements, Attributes, or Values Based on XPath Expressions

```
cat myfile.xml | xmlstarlet ed -d '/XPath_Expression'
```

Display Structure of XML File

```
xmlstarlet el -u myfile.xml
```

Pretty Print JSON Document

```
cat myfile.json | jq '.'
```

Pretty Print XML Document

```
cat myfile.xml | xmlstarlet fo
```

API (Application Programming Interface): Software interface that simplifies communication between applications.

argument: Information used by a command as input. In the example below, "hello world" is an argument to the echo command

```
echo "hello world"
```

array: Collections of the same type of variable that can be accessed through an index. In the example below, the "words" variable is broken into components where each word is an element in the "myarray" array. The first and third elements of myarray are then printed out.

```
words="word1 word2 word3"
myarray=$(words)
echo ${myarray[0]}
word1
echo ${myarray[1]}
word2
echo ${myarray[2]}
word3
```

command: An instruction that tells a computer to do something. In the example below, the echo command is used to print "hello world" to the screen.

```
echo "hello world"
```

command substitution: Allows the output of a command to be used as an argument for another command or be assigned to a variable

```
echo "Today is $(date +%A)"
```

CSV (Comma Separated Values): A delimited text format where a comma is used to separate fields

delimited text: Textual data where each line or entry represents a record and each field is separated by one or more characters.

escape character: A character that tells the computer the next character has special meaning. Escape characters are often used to render whitespace or unprintable characters. For example, `\n` indicates that a newline should be printed (rather than the letter n)

```
echo "Hello world.\nGoodbye cruel world" > mytest.txt
cat mytest.txt
```

Hello world.

Goodbye cruel world

JSON (JavaScript Object Notation): A simple text-based format for expressing and exchanging data.

Linked Open Data: Structured data that uses identifiers to express relationships between different items and concepts.

RDF (Resource Description Framework): Method for expressing relationships between things and concepts in XML.

regular expression: Special string of characters that allow search and replace based on patterns

REST (Representational State Transfer): Method for creating web services that programs interact with in a way that's similar to browsers

SGML (Standardized Generalized Markup Language): A set of rules developed in the 1960s that describe how to encode documents with text tags to make them machine-readable. SGML is a superset of XML and HTML.

string: Sequence of characters that may include letters, numbers, symbols, spaces, tabs, or any other Unicode character. In computer contexts, the words "string" and "text" are often used interchangeably.

turtle (Terse RDF Triple Language): A syntax for expressing data in RDF (Resource Description Framework)

Unicode: International encoding standard for text where each letter, number, character, or symbol is assigned a numeric value that can be interpreted on any computer platform.

XML (eXtensible Markup Language): Set of rules for encoding documents that are both human- and machine-readable.

XPath: Language for extracting specific data elements from XML elements and attributes.

> (greater than symbol): Directs the output into a file. If file already exists, content is replaced with output.

```
echo 'hello world'> mytestfile.txt
cat mytestfile.txt
```

>> (double greater than symbol): Appends the output of a command to a file

```
echo "hello world" > mytestfile.txt
echo "goodbye cruel world" >> mytestfile.txt
cat mytestfile.txt
```

| (pipe): Directs the output of a command to another command

```
echo -e "C is for Cat\nA is for Apple\nB is for
    Banana" |sort
```

A is for Apple

B is for Banana

C is for Cat

$(command) (Dollar sign and open paren followed by command and close paren): Allows command substitution so the output of command can be used as an argument for other commands or assigned to a variable.

```
echo "Today is $(date +%A)"
```

USEFUL COMMANDS

The following is a list of the most used commands and their primary purpose. More detailed information about usage complete with examples can be found in chapter 2.

awk: Manipulate and output data that is organized in rows and columns

cat (concatenate): Create and view files as well as redirect output to new files

cd (change directory): Change the working directory to the one specified

chmod (change mode): Change read, write, and execute permissions for files and directories.

```
chmod 666 testfile.txt
```

(make testfile.txt readable and writable by anyone)

column: Format input into columns. Useful for creating tables or working with fixed width data. column -t myfile

comm: Compares two files and indicates which lines are unique to each and which they have in common.

```
comm File1 File2
```

cp (copy): Copy files and directories.

```
cp -R /home/user1 .
```

(Recursively copy the /home/user directory and its contents to the current working directory)

curl: Retrieve and send data over a network.

date: Display and convert dates in a wide variety of formats.

```
date +%A
```

Thursday (displayed current day of the week)

```
echo "Three weeks from now is $(date--date '3 weeks'
    +'%A, %B %d'). This command can also normalize
    dates such as $(date -d 'march 8, 2018'
    +'%Y-%m-%d')"
```

Three weeks from now is Thursday, March 29. This command can also normalize dates such as 2018-03-08

(Shows date three weeks in future in user friendly format and converts text date to YYYY-MM-DD format. As of this writing, the date switch is not supported on Mac).

echo: Display text. Useful for creating customized output.

exiftool: Read and manipulate metadata in images, documents, videos, and other files

exit: Leave the current command line session. This will typically cause the window to close

find: Finds files based on virtually any criteria.

grep (global regular expression print): Searches for sophisticated patterns in text files or the output of other commands.

jq: Read and manipulate JSON.

key/value pair: Two values in which one designated as the "key" points to the value. For example, in the key/value pair

```
"Title" : "Migrating Library Data"
```

"Title" is the key that points to "Migrating Library Data." Programming languages use keys to access values.

less: View files of any size without opening them. Allows backward as well as forward movement through the file.

ln (link): Create a link to a file or directory.

ls (list): List directories and files.

mkdir (make directory): Create a directory.

mv (move): Move files and directories from one location to another. Moving a filename to another filename in the same directory renames it.

pwd (print working directory): Display the full pathname to the current working directory.

rm (remove): Delete files and directories.

sed (stream editor): Perform complex manipulation of data from programs or files.

sort: Sort files according to criteria you specify.

split: Split large files into smaller chunks.

string: Collections of characters that are typically numbers, letters, and punctuation. Text is string data.

sudo (super user do): Temporarily give the user elevated privileges to run administrative tasks such as installing new software.

tr (translate): Translate or delete characters.

uniq (unique): Identify unique or duplicated lines in files.

wc (word count): Count words, lines, and characters in a file.

xargs: Convert each line output from previous command to argument for next command.

xmlstarlet: Read and manipulate XML.

REGULAR EXPRESSION CHEAT SHEET

^	Match start of the line.
$	Match end of the line.
.	Match any single character.
*	Match zero or more of the previous character.
[A-D,G-J,0-5]*	Match zero or more of ABCDGHIJ012345.
[^A-C]	Match any one character that is *not* A,B, or C.
(dog)	Match the word "dog," including case, and remember that text to be used later in the match or replacement
\1	Insert the first remembered text as if it were typed here (\2 for second, \3 for third, etc.).
\	Use to match special characters or convert what is normally a special character to a regular character. For example, \w indicates a word character, \n indicates a newline, but \\ matches a backslash and * matches an asterisk.